Praise for

With winsome personal illustrations and a laser focus on the accurate understanding and application of God's Word, Kim brings readers to the throne of grace to experience God's glory for themselves on a daily basis. This is a wonderful resource for making time with the Lord a time of strengthening.

Tricia Scribner, PhD
Author of *LifeGivers Apologetics*

All devotionals are not cut from the same cloth. Typically light on God's Word and heavy on felt needs, they generally leave me unsatisfied. Rare is the devotional that is saturated in Scripture and rich in doctrine. Rarer still is the devotional actually devoted to living for the glory of God. Kim Kinney's *Living for His Glory* is such a rarity.

Kyler Smith, Ph.D.
Senior Associate Pastor
Hickory Grove Baptist Church in Charlotte, NC

This book is a beautiful call to a deep, meaningful, scriptural, and joyful walk with our Lord. His light shines brightly through these pages, radiating through the words—all pointing to His glory! Her topic-driven chapters are incredibly substantive and pragmatic with a firm foundation rooted in the totality and depth of scripture. The stories she intersperses make the message accessible and non-threatening. I believe other readers will experience joy in their reading, as I did.

Representative Kristin Baker, MD
NC State House

Kim has done an incredible job articulating what most disciples of Christ wrestle with and navigate on this journey of faith. With captivating stories and imagery, she brings biblical truths to life that all can relate to. Continually pointing readers back to true north, Kim reminds us that all aspects of our life are mere opportunities to catch glimpses of the glory of God. This book will challenge you to deeper faith and understanding of who God is and who He has called you to be.

Hannah Arrowood
Founder and Executive Director
Present Age Ministries

Living

for

His Glory

Kayla and Ellison –
You will both always be special
to me. Always live for God's glory;
nothing else matters.
With love,
Kim Kinney
Psalm 108:5

by Kim S. Kinney

Other Bible Translations Used

Scripture quotations labeled AMP are taken from the Amplified Bible, Copyright © 1954, 1958, 1962, 1964, 1965, 1987 by The Lockman Foundation. Used by permission.

—※—

Scripture quotations labeled CEB are from the Common English Bible © 2012 by Common English Bible or its suppliers. All rights reserved.

—※—

Scripture quotations labeled CEV are from the Contemporary English Version Copyright © 1991, 1992, 1995 by American Bible Society. Used by permission.

—※—

Scripture quotations labeled CSB, are taken from the Christian Standard Bible®, Copyright © 2016 by Holman Bible Publishers. Used by permission. Christian Standard Bible®, and CSB® is a federally registered trademark of Holman Bible Publishers

—※—

Scripture quotations labeled ESV are from The Holy Bible, English Standard Version®, copyright © 2001 by Crossway, a publishing ministry of Good News Publishers. Used by permission. All rights reserved.

—※—

All Scripture quotations marked KJV are from The King James Version.

—※—

Scripture quotations labeled MSG are from THE MESSAGE, copyright © 1993, 2002, 2018 by Eugene H. Peterson. Used by permission of NavPress, represented by Tyndale House Publishers. All rights reserved.

—※—

Scripture quotations labeled NASB are from the New American Standard Bible®, Copyright © 1960, 1971, 1977, 1995, 2020 by The Lockman Foundation. Used by permission. All rights reserved.

—※—

Scripture quotations labeled NCV are from the New Century Version®. Copyright © 2005 by Thomas Nelson. Used by permission. All rights reserved.

—※—

Scripture quotations labeled NIrV are from The Holy Bible, New International Reader's Version®, NIrV® Copyright © 1995, 1996, 1998, 2014 by Biblica, Inc.™ Used by permission of Zondervan. All rights reserved worldwide.

—※—

All Scripture quotations labeled NKJV are from the New King James Version®. Copyright © 1982 by Thomas Nelson. Used by permission. All rights reserved.

—※—

Scripture quotations labeled NLT are from the Holy Bible, New Living Translation, copyright ©1996, 2004, 2015 by Tyndale House Foundation. Used by permission of Tyndale House Publishers, Carol Stream, Illinois 60188. All rights reserved.

—※—

Scripture quotations labeled NRSV are from the New Revised Standard Version Bible, copyright © 1989 National Council of the Churches of Christ in the United States of America. Used by permission. All rights reserved worldwide.

—※—

Scripture quotations labeled TLB are from The Living Bible copyright © 1971. Used by permission of Tyndale House Publishers, All rights reserved.

Cover Inspiration

The sun is hidden, yet we see its rays bursting forth in dazzling brilliance along the fringes of the cloud.

We cannot see God this side of heaven; His full glory is too holy for our eyes to behold. Yet we see the radiance of His glory emanating with power from all directions of His being. It touches every aspect of our lives and changes everything!

Author's Note

For purposes of clarity and respect, I have taken the liberty of capitalizing all pronouns referring to the divinity, except for direct quotations from Scripture.

Dedication

I lovingly dedicate my first book to my beautiful family.

Bob, you are my biggest cheerleader and the source of my greatest encouragement. Without your unwavering support, this book would never have happened. You have never complained as I stayed glued to my computer hour upon hour. Thank you for sacrificing your study so I would have a secluded place for quiet contemplation and writing. Thank you for many hours of biblical discussion and for being my sounding board. I treasure those conversations and your insights. Your patience and love know no bounds.

Justin, you are the true wordsmith—the real author in the family, having published books of your own. You have been a source of inspiration to me and have been a great resource as the process to get from disjointed ideas to a published product is nothing less than completely daunting and overwhelming. Thank you for all your help. Your knowledge and endless assistance through my many challenges know no bounds.

Rebecca, you have been the patient encourager through a year and a half of challenges that hit repeatedly ever since I began writing. Your sense of humor when I became burdened by the weightiness of my subject matter has been a lifeline. Thank you for making me laugh and for understanding my frustrations. Your tender devotion and the quiet reminders of your love know no bounds.

Welcome

❧

G od's glory. Who can define it or grasp it in full measure? I don't pretend to have the answers or a sufficient understanding of the vastness of God's glory. This book contains divine inspirations from the Holy Spirit. My own knowledge and wisdom come up woefully short. But God…

I have bathed this book in prayer. If you glean anything of value as you read the words nestled within these pages, to Him be all glory. I am simply the vessel He used to convey biblical principles and insights.

This book contains works that I previously composed for Christian organizations or classes I taught to illustrate biblical concepts. Others are fresh writings for this book. Each chapter stands on its own. Topics and writing styles vary, yet it's all about His glory. Skip around, if you wish, using the topical index in the back. Or read straight through. Please note that scripture references are listed at the end of each chapter and bibliographical reference citations are recorded at the end of the book.

I trust that God has something here to appeal to everyone and to address each reader's spiritual needs. It is my prayer that you enjoy what you read, but mostly that you draw closer to God as you ponder what it means to live for His glory. May you be blessed as you read these pages. May we journey to the divine depths of His grace and mercy as we embrace all that He has for us. I'm glad I'm not alone on this journey. Let's begin together.

Kim S. Kinney

Contents

Introduction

At some point, we all circle around to these questions, "Why am I here?" and "What is the purpose of my life?"

As we go about our mundane, daily existence, we begin to wonder: What's the point? And the point is this: It's not about us. Nothing in this world or in this life is about us. It's all about God. God is the point. We aren't the point. And that's a very good thing!

Let's back up a bit. If you open the Bible and start to read on page one, the very first words are extremely important: "In the beginning God…" (Genesis 1:1). God was there in the beginning—the very beginning—before there was anything at all, except God. That's because God preexisted all of creation. Notice there is no mention of you and me in these pages. That's because we didn't exist! It was all about God. And it still is. He created the world and everything in it. Why? *For His glory.* God created *everything* for His glory. The whole earth is filled with His glory. All of creation points to God and reveals His glory.

Do you want to know this God of glory? One way we can learn more about God is to observe His creation—the orchestration of His majesty in nature and all He created. Through creation, we can discern God's eternal power and holiness. By actively watching and interacting with creation, we grow in knowledge of and relationship with God as He reveals Himself and His majesty to us.

So where do we come in? God made man and woman in His image.

Living for His *Glory*

God created mankind in his own image,
in the image of God he created them;
male and female he created them.
Genesis 1:27

Not only are we part of His magnificent creation but are the *crowning achievement* of His creation because we are crafted in God's image. Let this fact embrace your soul! Once we fully grasp the enormous magnitude of this, we won't live life the same way ever again.

As such, we weren't created to live self-directed lives for our own moments of glory. That would be selling ourselves desperately short. Our glory is so trivial and insignificant! We must look higher—beyond ourselves—because our purpose is far greater! Pastor Paul David Tripp once said, "If you are in Christ, you've been chosen to transcend the borders of your own glory, to reach out toward a greater glory, the glory of God."[A] We are to live for *God's* glory. Our lives should glorify Him. Everything we do should reflect His glory and point people to "the LORD Almighty—the King of glory" (Psalm 24:10).

All well and good, but let's face it: our lives reflect the God we perceive Him to be, not who He really is. Who do we believe God is? It all comes down to how well we know Him. And we know Him in direct proportion to the amount of time we spend in His presence. Do we believe God does great things? Or do we believe His impact is really very little? If we believe the latter, then our purpose here will be little and our reflection of Him quite inconsequential. But if we believe God is glory itself—filled with majesty and honor—then our lives take on far more significant meaning and purpose.

We should manifest His magnificent glory—not just in the big moments of life, but also in the small, seemingly insignificant moments. We were created to be instruments of His glory to tell His story. Whatever we do (eat, sleep, run errands, work, interact with people, serve, clean our homes, care for ourselves and our bodies, love our families, love others), we are called to do it for the glory of God as a way to honor him.[1]

This gives our lives divine purpose and every task heavenly importance. When we live in this way, our daily lives become sweet and pleasing worship of our Creator. The way we live our lives reverberates for eternity and its impact is incalculable.

We didn't evolve from the slime in some primordial swamp. We were lovingly handcrafted in a very intentional way by a holy God. We were given skills and talents for the purpose of serving Him. Everything about our lives should exalt and glorify God. This is the ultimate goal and our greatest purpose and privilege.

It is my prayer that the Holy Spirit will reveal Himself through the pages of this book and show us what it looks like to live our lives for God's utmost glory.

There is no greater honor.

---

[1] 1 Corinthians 10:31 – Whether you eat or drink or whatever you do, do it all for the glory of God.

We do not segment our lives, giving some time to God, some to our business or schooling, while keeping parts to ourselves. The idea is to live all of our lives in the presence of God, under the authority of God, and for the honor and glory of God. That is what the Christian life is all about.

R. C. Sproul

I'm dead in the water if I can't see the all-sufficient glory of God.

Louie Giglio

If you don't feel strong desires for the manifestation of the glory of God, it is not because you have drunk deeply and are satisfied. It is because you have nibbled so long at the table of the world. Your soul is stuffed with small things, and there is no room for the great.

John Piper

1

⎯⌇⎯

One Story

Many of us look at the Bible as 66 individual books. Which book should I read next? In which book is that scripture? What book of the Bible should I study? But the Bible should really be regarded as one book, complete from beginning to end.

It all started in a garden paradise where Adam and Eve saw God every day; they talked with Him and walked with Him. And they ate from the Tree of Life. Then one day everything changed in an instant when sin entered in. Eden was never the same. And access to Eden was barred.

Out of Adam and Eve came numerous generations and we read the history of the Jewish people with their many failings. We see the way God brought healing from their brokenness, redemption from their sin, and restoration to achieve His purposes. The five major and twelve minor prophets predicted over 1800 prophecies,[A] hundreds of which have come true and many awaiting God's perfect timing for their fulfillment. They prophesied the rise and fall of dynasties and the fate of individuals—all pointing toward Jesus. Of greatest significance, they predicted 48 prophecies about Jesus (plus 324 more relating to Him) exactly as told in scripture, revealing the holy inspiration of Scripture and God's divine plan for this world.

The four gospels are biographical books written about the life and ministry of Jesus and lay the foundation for

Christianity. Paul's thirteen letters and the eight general epistles speak of the Christian faith and display Christian doctrine. Every New Testament book refers back to Jesus.

And this one story culminates in Revelation when God will restore this broken world back to that garden paradise. And He will bring us there; only it will be better. It will be perfect, and the Tree of Life will be larger such that it will be on both sides of the river of the water of life. It will bear exquisite fruit every month.[1] We will walk with God, talk with Him, and see Him every day in perfect relationship.

God was at the beginning of history because He created it: mankind, the garden, and all we know. And He was there in the middle of the story: through the battles, family dysfunction, and tremendous brokenness. And God will be at the end of history as He brings eternal salvation to believers and His just judgment on this fallen world. He holds history, the present, and the future in the palm of His hand.

> I am the Alpha and the Omega,
> The First and the Last,
> the Beginning and the End.[2]

One complete book. One triune God. From the beginning in Genesis, through the prophets' prediction of the Messiah, to the coming of Jesus in the gospels, and finally His ultimate return in Revelation. One story from beginning to end. It all points to Jesus. It glorifies Him and Him alone.

---

[1] Revelation 22:2B - On each side of the river stood the tree of life, bearing twelve crops of fruit, yielding its fruit every month.

[2] Revelation 22:13

2

⌒

Our Integrity is our Legacy

*P*astor Greg Laurie tells the story of a pastor who boarded a bus one Monday morning, paid his fare, and found a seat. As he examined his coins, he realized the driver had given him too much change. Many people would have kept it, thanking God for His favor. But this pastor was convicted. At the next stop, he returned the extra change to the driver, saying, "Excuse me, sir, you gave me too much change and I wanted to return it to you, because obviously you made a mistake."

The driver replied, "Pastor, I didn't make a mistake. I was at your church last night and heard you preach on honesty. I wanted to see if you practiced what you preach." Thankfully, this pastor did.[A]

When people find out you're a Christian, they will watch you very carefully. They will analyze and scrutinize your every move. Christian speaker, Carolyn Mahaney notes:

> Our conduct has a direct influence on how people think about the gospel. The world doesn't judge us by our theology; the world judges us by our behavior. People don't necessarily want to know what we believe about the Bible. They want to see if what we believe makes a difference in our lives. Our actions either bring glory to God or misrepresent His truth.

People want to know if you are different—if your actions mimic your words. Evangelist D.L. Moody noted that "Out of 100 people outside the church, one might read the Bible, but 99 will read the Christian." The way you live your life matters. People are watching you. And truthfully, most people want to see you fail. They want to know this Christian walk isn't what it's cracked up to be so they can continue living as they have been—in sin and selfishness. When they see that you are different—truly different—it will rock their world to its core.

"Wrong is always wrong, even if *everybody* does it. And conversely, right is right, even if *nobody* does it!"[B] Personal integrity is something we are fine tuning every time we think a thought and every time we act. Who are you when no one is looking? This reflects your integrity.

If you could look in the mirror and see not your face, but your integrity, would you look or be too afraid? In the end, when we stand before a holy God, everything will be laid open and exposed. Our integrity will be on full display.

Nothing in all creation is hidden from God's sight.
Everything is uncovered and laid bare before
the eyes of him to whom we must give account.
Hebrews 4:13

Job was a man who lived his life for God, honoring Him in all he did. Although he was very wealthy and had many blessings, he never allowed his money or advantages to control him. He submitted to God and allowed his faith to steer him.

Job... was honest,
a person of absolute integrity.
Job 1:1a, CEB

Even when Satan assaulted him with one calamity after another, Job responded in an upright manner, never cursing God. Despite extreme suffering, Job chose to live for His glory, stating with courage,

> Let me be weighed on honest scales,
> That God may know my integrity.
> Job 31:6, NKJV

Despite one tragedy after another, Job guarded his integrity with diligence. What a superb example for us. God doesn't expect us to live perfect lives, but to strive to live blamelessly,[1] no matter our circumstances, always glorifying Him with our behavior. And when we fall short, God's grace will compassionately catch us as we confess our shortcomings. His mercies are new every morning.[2]

Guard it well

Austin Phelps, a minister and president of Andover Theological Seminary, wisely noted that our integrity "is the only thing we can take with us into eternity." We are responsible for our integrity; it doesn't just happen. Each day, we are either growing our integrity or tearing it down. It is built over time, piece by piece, with every choice we make. Every situation we encounter is an opportunity to build our integrity. Our integrity reflects our faith, our beliefs, and our worldview. If we profess faith in our holy God, we reflect His character in everything we do and say. We must carefully guard and protect our integrity; this is our witness to a watching world. What a daunting responsibility.

We are daily confronted with opportunities to take the easy path, at the risk of our integrity. Christian composer,

M.H. McKee observed, "Wisdom is knowing the right path to take...Integrity is taking it." Don't gamble with your honor and opt for the path of least resistance; it is never worth it. It takes years to build an honorable integrity, yet only a second to lose. Guard it with all you've got.

We all leave behind a spiritual legacy when we die, whether favorable or not. Our integrity is the spiritual legacy we pass down to our children and descendants. The integrity of a good name and a life well-lived is beyond compare.

> The righteous man walks in his integrity;
> His children are blessed after him.
> Proverbs 20:7, NKJV

What an invaluable gift for those who follow in our footsteps. And what a remarkable way to glorify God.

---

[1] Psalm 119:1a - Blessed are those whose ways are blameless.
[2] Lamentations 3:22b-23a, ESV - His mercies never come to an end; they are new every morning.

3

God is in the Winds

*P*ilots will tell you that one of the first lessons on aerodynamics they learn is to turn their plane into a headwind. As the fast gusts of air bear down on the plane, it generates a force on the wings that propels the plane upward, lifting it off the ground to higher sights.

How did pilots learn this? Years ago, they studied the birds. If a bird is flying for fun, it goes with the wind, gliding with delight. But if the bird faces danger, it turns into the wind which causes it to rise quickly, escaping the threat, as it soars toward the sun.

Are you struggling right now? Are you in a storm—engulfed in darkness and the harsh winds of oppression and opposition? Do you find that every step you take comes with great effort—and you can hardly make it through the day, much less get off the ground? Do you feel like running away? Don't. Don't run from the storm. Turn around and face it head on. In Christ's strength, you will rise above it as you soar toward the Son.

As believers, God assures us we are never alone. He is with us: indwelling us, guiding us, strengthening us, and comforting us. Run toward the storm and you will find Christ waiting for you—ready to lift you up to greater heights. Rest in Him and allow Him to carry you through the storm[1] to a greater promise.

Living for His *Glory*

I will cause you to ride in triumph
on the heights of the land...
Isaiah 58:14b

Have you ever witnessed a summer storm? Picture an oppressively hot and muggy day. The sultry air is suffocating. Perspiration beads on your brow as you move through the thick, stifling atmosphere. As you look up, you notice a cloud in the distance. You watch as it grows dark, gaining momentum as it rolls with increasing force across the heavens, joining with other clouds in its midst. The clouds swell and thicken. A wind picks up. Without warning, a bright flash of light zigzags its way across the heavens as thunder pierces the expanse above with jarring intensity, shattering the sky with power. Suddenly, the clouds burst open with a downpour of rain. The temperature drops and a pelting deluge surges down from above.

Eventually the storm passes and the sun peeks through the sky, casting light and a freshness all around. Often, we are treated to a glorious rainbow. The humidity has eased; the temperature has dropped. You feel a sense of relief as you look up, able to breathe and move with less effort.

The world has changed. The grass is brighter. The heaviness has lifted. The temperature is cooler, no longer oppressive. It is refreshing. It is freeing. It is exhilarating. God knows when something beautiful in the future necessitates going through a difficult storm in the present.

Storms, although powerful and threatening, don't last forever. Your storm will pass; the rain will stop, and sunshine will break through the clouds. The world will have changed. It will feel liberating, and you will be stronger for having weathered the tempest.

God is in Every Tomorrow
by Laura A. Barter Snow

God is in every tomorrow,
Therefore I live for today;
Certain of finding at sunrise
Guidance and strength for the day,

Power for each moment of weakness,
Hope for each moment of pain
Comfort for every sorrow,
Sunshine and joy after rain.

God is in every tomorrow,
Planning for you and for me.
Even in the dark I will follow,
Trust where my eyes cannot see.

Stilled by His promise of blessing,
Soothed by the touch of His hand.
Confident in His protection,
Knowing my life-path is planned.

May God bless you and hold you in the palm of His hand as you weather the storm. He sees you. This storm didn't take Him by surprise. He will carry you through. His grace will provide everything you need.

Blessings and beauty often follow storms. Hang on. Better times coming…

---

[1] Isaiah 46:4 – Even to your old age and gray hairs I am he, I am he who will sustain you. I have made you and I will carry you; I will sustain you and I will rescue you.

4

Sudden Storms

It was a beautiful, tranquil day in Madison, Wisconsin. The ravishing sky of summer was cloaked in a shrine of neon blues. Glimmers of sunlight danced on the rippling waters of Lake Mendota as a friend and I set sail one relaxing afternoon. I had grown up sailing, so I was comfortable renting a boat and embarking on a passage through the shimmering sapphire Wisconsin waters. We were having a grand time skimming over the water as we raced to the outer reaches of the area. After a while, above the continuous lapping of the waters over the hull of our boat, I could barely hear a foghorn-type of sound in the distance. I didn't know what the sound meant, but no matter, it didn't diminish our fun.

As time went on, we noticed the wind picking up. I trimmed the sheets so the sails became taut, creating the lift I was seeking. What a blast we were having, slicing through the water as the wind filled our sails, propelling us forward at an exhilarating pace! As we slowed to turn, we suddenly noticed the clouds seemed more abundant. Quite gray, in fact. Ominous even.

I nervously looked around. We had been having such a great time that we failed to notice the warning signs. Where the sailboats and other watercraft had been plentiful when we started our excursion, we now seemed to be the only craft out. "We better head in," I exclaimed anxiously. My friend eagerly agreed. Then the rain burst forth through the dark veil of clouds gathered above. In no time, we were being assaulted with swollen drops of blustery precipitation. The mast swayed forcefully as the wind quickly gained momentum. A wave crashed into the shiny wood of the hull, soaking us in the surge.

With a new intensity, I wiped the rain from my eyes and began tacking back and forth as fast as I could in order to reach shore safely. Fear swelled up inside me, although I tried to hide the mounting tension I acutely felt. I focused on the task ahead, using the wind to our advantage without allowing it to rip apart the sails as we steered toward safety.

As I navigated the boat to the dock through the pelting deluge, I felt a growing sense of relief the closer we got to shore. Finally, we made it! The shore crew informed us that the foghorn warnings were meant for us—alerting us of the impending storm. Yet we were unaware and ignored them to our peril. Thankfully, all ended well—God was merciful—and a valuable lesson was learned.

Personal storms

Perhaps you are facing a challenge. Life had been going quite well. Days were beautiful. Peace had reigned. Yet, while you were busy living, not paying much attention, the climate abruptly changed. A storm came out of nowhere and now you are trying to navigate as best you can. The fast-moving clouds seem to grow continually more menacing day after day, as the sky darkens. The wind is picking up and the rain is starting to fall. You, my friend, are navigating a spiritual storm.

We will all face many storms in our lives; there will be no scarcity. Jesus even warns us that we will encounter troubles, but only after reassuring us that He will provide the peace to endure and master the storm.

> I have told you these things,
> so that in me you may have peace.
> In this world you will have trouble.
> But take heart! I have overcome the world.
> John 16:33

Peace first. Trouble second. And when we submit, God's divine peace will be there to get us through.

Sometimes, we are the cause of the mess in which we find ourselves. We are busy having fun, heading into a storm, yet there are warnings—equivalent to the foghorn I chose to ignore that day on the lake. I was so absorbed in doing my thing, that I failed to look around—until it was too late. At that point, the wind was already raging, and the rain was tumbling down with fury.

I could have avoided all this if I had only looked around and noted the warnings. What does your storm look like? Perhaps it all started out as fun. A relationship that was carefree—until it wasn't; it started exerting pressures you knew were wrong. Perhaps it was a glass of wine from time to time, but now it's every day—and you seem to crave the sensation of the cool liquid slipping down your throat. Maybe it was thrilling at first to light a joint and take a couple of long, lazy tokes. But now it's more—much more. Or perhaps shopping and spending money on a few indulgences was fun and liberating to begin with, but now you can't stop yourself. Amazon packages keep coming. And the bills are mounting. Or maybe it's far more than that. Possibly the first rolls of the dice were exhilarating, the bets holding promise, but now you're running cold, the stakes are too high, too many folds, and you're in deep.

Are you having a hard time staying afloat? Were there people who tried to talk with you beforehand? Friends who cared? Family who seemed worried? Beneath the bravado, you were really a bit nervous, yet you ruthlessly dismissed the cold feet.

Franklin D. Roosevelt once said, "A smooth sea never made a skilled sailor." Sometimes God allows the winds of adversity and the storms of our own carelessness to teach us lessons we desperately need and to grow our faith. That day on the lake taught me a valuable lesson I won't forget. I never made that mistake again.

―――

Do not fear the tempest
nor shrink back as the wind pounds.
Don't cower in the blinding hail
nor tremble as the thunder sounds.
Don't panic as you look above
the ominous, rolling clouds abound.
Don't get flustered at the chaos
of the storm surge that surrounds.

Look instead and see your Savior
in the eye of the storm.
When you are frightened and feel hopeless
your cherished spirit He'll transform.
As He wraps you with His comfort
in your fears His peace will form.
In His timing cease the mighty squall.
He's the perfect calm in the storm.[A]

―――

Regardless of your storm, if you are a Christian, you have a definite advantage over unbelievers. You are never alone. God is in the storm. You can overcome your troubles and the worldly stress as you rely on your faith in Jesus, the Son of God.[1] Will you allow Him to take the bad and grow you through it?

We will all face storms in this life—many storms. Don't submit to the storm in despair and defeat. Realize how far out to sea you've drifted and turn around; aim the bow toward shore and head directly back to safety—with no excursions along the way. Don't miss the fact that while the storm may be all that you can see, that's not all there is. Beyond the storm and the billowing, steely gray clouds is the dazzling radiance of His divine glory.

> Though I am surrounded by troubles,
> you will bring me safely through them.
> Psalm 138:7a, TLB

---

[1] 1 John 5:5 – Who is it that overcomes the world? Only the one who believes that Jesus is the Son of God.

5

~~

Imprisoned

The apostle Paul led a fascinating life. He influenced Christianity, and maybe the world, more than any other man, except for Jesus Christ. He spread the gospel throughout the Roman Empire and wrote 13 (possibly 14) books of the Bible.

Born in AD 5, he probably died around AD 68. During his lifetime, Paul suffered greatly for his faith and the cause of Christ. However, nothing deterred him from spreading the gospel and advancing the kingdom. He was arrested several times for preaching his Christian faith and was eventually sent to Rome at the end of his life. He had a preliminary hearing which didn't go well and he was thrown into a dreadful dungeon cell of the Mamertine Prison and placed in chains.[A]

Few prisons were as hideous, filthy, dank, and dreary as the lower chamber Paul occupied. Prisoners were rarely sent to that prison as punishment, but rather were held there as they awaited trial or the death sentence. Paul didn't expect to be acquitted. He was confident he would be found guilty and would face execution.[B]

The prison

To get some perspective, let's zero in on the type of prison that housed Paul. Prisons of that day were very primitive. They were damp, dark, cold, and without any comforts whatsoever. Prisoners slept on the hard floor or, if fortunate, on a rough pallet on the floor.[C]

Paul was chained to a Roman guard which prevented his escape. The manner of the chains varied. Prisoners were chained to one or both legs, one or both wrists, or around the neck. The chains were made of rough iron, not polished like chains we use today. They would eventually rust with the perspiration of the prisoners, especially in the summer months. Each chain weighed about 15 pounds. They were noisy and creaked with any movement, making sleep extremely challenging.[C]

The burden of getting food fell on the shoulders of the prisoners. To depend on prison food was risky. Prisoners received about half the amount of food given to slaves. The food barely sustained life and was often withheld as a means of torture.[C] Many prisons didn't supply any food at all, so prisoners were at the mercy of what food friends and family brought them.

Prisoners lacked good hygiene through no fault of their own. Baths were unlikely. Because no knives were allowed, prisoners couldn't cut their hair. They had to put up with long, uncombed, and matted hair, often infested with lice. Clothes were seldom washed and became completely soiled.[C]

Ventilation was very poor, and the prisoners often died for lack of air or from temperature extremes. Dead bodies were piled in corners to be taken away later.[C] The stench was overwhelming. Rats and vermin were common.[D]

Prisons had little natural light. During the night, it was complete and total darkness, the mental impact of which was maddening.[C]

Isolation

Many friends deserted Paul in his time of need for fear of persecution. Only Luke remained. Paul knew he was facing death. He wasn't dying of a disease in a sterile hospital with modern conveniences, pain medicine, and loved ones gathered nearby. He lay in the most dreaded of Roman prisons, cut off from the world with Luke as his only visitor.

This prison was isolated—actually difficult to locate. Paul's cell had an 18-inch square hole in the ceiling through which everything passed into or out of the cell, including his second letter to Timothy.[A] Imagine Paul's despair and fear. But he didn't complain; his primary concern was advancement of the gospel at all costs.

This was the backdrop

Paul wrote his final letter, 2 Timothy, from this prison. Timothy, a young man, had become like a son to him. He had been leading the church in Ephesus for four years at the time.[E] Paul asked Timothy to come right away, not knowing if he would arrive before he was executed. And Paul issued a special request at the end of the chapter. As you know, people's last words are often worth listening to. Let's look more closely at his request.

When you come, bring the cloak…
and my scrolls, especially the parchments.
2 Timothy 4:13

Paul had likely not been allowed to gather his personal belongings when he was thrown into the dungeon.

His cloak

The Greek word for cloak, *phailonen*, does not occur anywhere else in the NT. It was similar to a modern-day poncho. It was like a heavy blanket fashioned in a circular shape with a hole cut in the center for the head.[F] Cloaks were usually made of wool, sometimes leather.[G]

His cloak could also be used as bedding as it was more comfortable than sleeping on the bare floor. In the winter, prisoners used their cloaks more like a sleeping bag, sleeping on one half and wrapping the other half around them like a blanket.[G] This cloak was likely the only coat Paul owned and winter was coming. The prison was damp and chilly. Imagine his sense of urgency. Next-day shipping didn't exist; there was no Amazon Prime. The process of receiving the cloak would take weeks as Ephesus was over 1200 miles away.

Paul's cloak represented his physical needs.

His scrolls and parchments

Paul asked for the scrolls. The Greek word for scrolls was *biblia*. It means "books." It is from this word that we get the word, "Bible." The scrolls were rolls of papyrus. These could have contained the Torah or other Old Testament writings.[G]

But Paul especially wanted the parchments. The Greek word for parchments was *membranas*. The parchment manuscripts were made from skins of sheep or goats. They were very thin, specially treated leather.[G]

These precious parchments were probably copies of Old Testament books, the gospels, or perhaps copies of his own letters. They could have even contained blank sheets on which he could write more letters. Interestingly, the literacy rate in Israel at that time was probably less than 3%.[H]

Paul was not going to waste his time in prison. He was going to spend his time learning, strengthening his faith, advancing the kingdom, and bolstering his courage with encouragement from God's Word. (Interestingly, the word "encouragement" has "courage" as its root. When a friend encourages us, he builds us up with courage.)

Paul's scrolls and parchments represented his spiritual needs.

A very bleak and desolate time

Paul was living through a very dark time with no hope for escape. It's safe to assume he was cold, bored, lonely for his friends, exhausted, hungry, and anxious. Suffering any of these conditions makes us vulnerable to the wiles of Satan who will take full advantage of any of our weaknesses. It's perfectly understandable that Paul turned to his dear friend, Timothy, and requested something for his physical needs as well as something for his spiritual needs.

Timothy did make it to Rome, but we have no idea if he made it in time to see Paul alive. If he did, he likely witnessed Paul's death. Paul was beheaded in Rome, probably in May or June AD 68, with a sword.[A] Imagine how upsetting this had to have been for Timothy.

Our own prison

Some crisis happens and we are thrown into the clutches of fear and misery as we enter our own prison of sorts. The conditions are atrocious. We can't sleep. We feel lonely and isolated. Breathing can be difficult (just like Paul must have struggled with breathing in the poor ventilation of the prison). We don't know where to turn. We don't know how to escape or get relief. Hope evaporates. We feel we may not survive.

Although it must have seemed like it at times, Paul was never alone; Jesus was with him in his prison, and he knew what Paul was going through; Jesus was in control.

Jesus is there with you in your prison as well, whatever your prison may be. He knows what you're going through and is in control, whether it feels like it or not.

Don't panic. Satan has temporarily gained the upper hand as he has managed to send you into your own personal prison of gloom and fear. Your crisis happened suddenly; that's his modus operandi. Do NOT allow Satan to be in control. Focus on the presence of Jesus and ignore Satan. Do not curl up in despair.

Physical needs

What do you physically need to help you cope? Eat well. Sleep. Exercise. Make healthy choices. Put together a budget. Be prepared. Talk with doctors. Make the appointment. Sometimes we need to call on trusted family or friends to help us. Paul sought help from Timothy. Who are your Timothys? Our family and friends are gifts from God to help us in our times of need. Don't overlook what they can offer. Look around; I bet you have several people who will gladly come to your aid if you make them aware of your situation.

Spiritual needs

What do you spiritually need to help you cope? Where is your Bible? Read it; it is alive and active[1] and will encourage you. Keep a divine perspective. God will never leave you. He never says, "You go and I'll wait here." He says, "Let's go!"

Obeying God's Word brings strength and courage. Go to church. Do you need Christian counseling? Get what you need. If God is allowing this situation, He will enable you to deal with it successfully in His strength.

People say we are bodies with a soul. I disagree. I believe we are souls with a body. Our souls are eternal; our bodies are temporary. As such, our spiritual needs come first, then our physical needs.

God tells you to be strong and have courage. Will you listen to His voice or the voice of defeat? Your choice determines who wins the battle for your mind. Will you follow the gods of this world and live with fear or follow God and His Word and live with faith?

Fear or faith? Whichever you choose will rule you.

It's time to give Satan his final notice and regain control. What is the worst that can happen? Whatever life holds for you, even if you are facing death, you will come out on top if you are a Christian. Ironically, death is the ultimate victory.

> Death has been swallowed up in victory.
> Where, O death, is your victory?
> Where, O death, is your sting?
> Thanks be to God! He gives us the victory
> through our Lord Jesus Christ.
> 1 Corinthians 15:54b-55, 57

As Paul lived his last days in the Roman prison, he likely remembered words from a previous prison epistle he wrote. "For to me, to live is Christ and to die is gain."[2] Paul had his priorities right. He lived by faith, secure in the knowledge that God was in control. If he survived, he would live to bring glory to God, even in his suffering. But if it should be time for him to die, his death would also bring glory to God. Paul knew that what we lose in life, we gain in heaven. And what a gain for him personally as he would live with his Savior forever, face to face in glory.

---

[1] Hebrews 4:12

[2] Philippians 1:21

6

Spiritual Thirst

We aren't told her name. I suppose it's not important. She lived in Samaria and one day she was making her daily trek to a well—Jacob's Well—in the middle of the day. All alone. This was the hottest part of the day. Women went to the well for water in the early mornings and evenings. But this woman was excluded. Shunned. So she came alone. Every day.

This woman was lugging a heavy, cumbersome jug. It was awkward—hard to carry. Yet she trudged ahead; she needed water after all.

On this particular day, she was surprised to see a man sitting down beside the well. Even more surprised when he spoke with her. He was obviously Jewish, which is important to note, because in that day, the Jews literally hated the Samaritans and didn't talk with them. The Samaritans were considered half breeds—half Assyrian and half Jewish. (The Assyrians were the evil archenemies of the Jews.) This man asked her for water; in doing so, He put himself subservient to her. Men didn't speak with women in public and rabbis especially didn't speak with women in public, not even their wives, mothers, or sisters. But this man was Jesus and He asked her for a favor.

This woman was confused and asked Him why He was speaking with her. He mentioned that He had living water. This baffled her as she considered the well's water. She knew that he'd have to dig at least 100 feet down to reach the spring that fed the well. Not a small, nor easy, task.

> "Sir," the woman said, "you have nothing to draw with and the well is deep. Where can you get this living water?"
> Jesus answered, "Everyone who drinks this water will be thirsty again, but whoever drinks the water I give them will never thirst. Indeed, the water I give them will become in them a spring of water welling up to eternal life."
> John 4:11, 13-14

Jesus asked her to call her husband and she replied honestly, admitting she had none. He told her she was right; she had had five husbands and was now living with another man. They talked a bit, then Jesus revealed His identity to her. He was the Messiah.

Her mouth dropped open in astonishment; her eyes grew wide in wonder. She believed Him and was so elated that she ran back to town, leaving her water jug behind, to tell the others about Jesus, the Messiah, who met her at the well. She freely and unabashedly shared her joy of Jesus and didn't worry about the response.

> Many of the Samaritans from that town believed in him because of the woman's testimony.
> John 4:39a

This woman had a bad reputation. She was neither liked nor respected. But the people listened to her testimony— and women *and* men believed because of her.

She left her cumbersome water jug behind because she was now filled with living water. The jug suddenly became unnecessary.

What are your jugs—your wells?

What jugs are you lugging around, day after day after day? What burdens are you carrying? This woman had a HUGE hole inside that she tried to fill with the attention of men. What holes in your heart and in your life are you trying to fill to feel better—or to just survive?

Which wells are you pursuing to fill your jugs: the wells of worldly success, of money, of approval, of popularity, of materialism, or of pleasure, perhaps? Apart from Jesus, we will thirst again because the wells of this world all lead to spiritual thirst. They will run dry. Every—Single—Time.

Let's leave our heavy, burdensome jugs at the feet of Jesus like this woman did. They aren't necessary anymore because there's no need to return to the worldly wells.

Like this Samaritan woman, we can become so intent on meeting our immediate needs that we miss God's hand reaching out to us in love with what we *truly* need. Only Christ can fill our empty souls for eternity and provide for our fractured emotional needs.

Remember what this woman did. When she found living water, she left her jug (which represented her old life) behind and told people about Jesus. She shared her testimony—her interaction with Jesus. And many believed. It's that simple. (Please read the full story in John 4:1-42.)

We all have a testimony. And Jesus commands us to tell others about Him; it's called the Great Commission.

Go and make disciples of all nations.
Matthew 28:19a

We aren't to worry about the response. God will reap the harvest. The way you use your abilities and talents to share your testimony is reflected in:

- How you love others
- How you live your life
- How you talk about Jesus
- How you extend grace and forgiveness
- How you invite people to church or Bible Study
- How you serve
- The language you use
- The TV shows and movies you watch
- The books you read
- How you spend money
- How you react to situations
- How you deal with anger
- Whether you gossip
- How you vote
- How you respond to persecution
- How you care for one another's children

Jesus is calling

Are you hurting? Broken? Alone? Are you exhausted and drained from returning to your sin—over and over again? Do you thirst for a drink from the well? Jesus is calling out to you. He offers living water. How will you respond? He is not asking you to do extraordinary things. Will you turn from your sin? Will you tell others about Jesus? That's what this woman from Samaria did. And God includes her in the Bible. She was found faithful. And she was valued.

7

But Even if He Does Not…

In May 2013, our family had the incredible privilege of joining a Bible study tour of Israel and Jordan with Jim and Pam Reimann. This was the 26th and final Bible-teaching tour they led. These tours were enhanced by the depth of Jim's knowledge of biblical history and his many experiences in the Holy Land. At each stop, we opened our Bibles and lost ourselves in Jim's moving storytelling and brilliant teaching of historical events that occurred where we were standing or upon the landscape which held us entranced. As Jim unfolded each nuance of the story or event he shared with us, we were mesmerized, captivated by the gravity of what we were hearing. It was sometimes overwhelming to process the significance of every historical detail. One thing we all knew; we were on holy ground. The way Jim brought the Bible to life in the land where it was written was incredible and awe-inspiring!

Jim Reimann was an ordained minister, author, and editor with over 6 million copies of his books in print. He edited and updated these great works (adding his commentary to the last two):

- *My Utmost for His Highest* by Oswald Chambers
- *Streams in the Desert* by Lettie Cowman
- *Morning by Morning* by Charles Spurgeon
- *Evening by Evening* by Charles Spurgeon

A few months later, Jim began displaying disturbing deficits in cognition and memory. After numerous medical tests, he was diagnosed with Creutzfeldt-Jakob (KROITS-felt YAH-kob) disease (CJD) which is a degenerative brain disorder. It is rapidly progressive and always fatal. Most patients die within 6-12 months of the first symptoms. (Jim's disease progressed much more quickly.) There is no cure. It is extremely rare, affecting about one person in every one million per year worldwide.[A]

On November 15th, shortly before Jim lost the ability to speak, his friend of 40 years came to visit him. His friend, a pastor, had been reading the book of Daniel. As he read aloud chapter 3, the Lord laid some insights on his heart which he wanted to share with Jim. Interestingly, the Lord had laid these exact verses on Jim's heart as well.

> Shadrach, Meshach, and Abednego replied
> to him, "King Nebuchadnezzar,
> we do not need to defend ourselves
> before you in this manner.
> If we are thrown into the blazing furnace,
> the God we serve is able to deliver us from it,
> and he will deliver us from Your Majesty's hand.
> But even if he does not, we want you to know,
> Your Majesty, that we will not serve your gods or
> worship the image of gold you have set up."
> Daniel 3:16-18

Jim shared with him, "I know that God is able to save me from CJD and rescue me from the suffering, but even if he does not, I will not bow to the god of disbelief, the god of fear, or the god of doubt." Jim asked that this be shared at his funeral. Jim trusted God throughout all the suffering and the fear he must have experienced. His faith and trust never wavered. He submitted fully to God's will, choosing to glorify God no matter what happened.

As he battled this dreadful disease, his family consistently prayed "for God's will so that He may be glorified through all of this."[B] Four days before he died, Jim went into a coma. Just before he died, Jim raised himself up in bed with a profoundly peaceful countenance and looked up. He then dropped back on his pillow and died with his wife and all three adult children beside him. This was December 18, 2013, less than five weeks after his friend visited. Jim was only 63.

His family was comforted by looking back at many of the writings that had come from Jim's pen, as recorded in two of his books, *Morning by Morning* and *Evening by Evening*. Here is a brief sampling:[B]

- When it comes to sickness, we must keep in mind there may be a purpose greater than our own – that God may be glorified!

- It is not God's will for everyone to be healed each and every time we pray for healing. If that were truly the case, we would never see a believer die physically, and we know that occurs. Of course, when we see a friend or family member dealing with a difficult illness, our spiritual nature leads us to pray for them. And that is what we should do. Yet we must keep in mind that our will always must be in submission to God's will.

- So many Christians fear death, but in truth a believer never really dies. Otherwise, eternal life would not be eternal. And if we think about it, do we really want to live forever in these earthly bodies, facing continual weakening, decline, and decay? Perhaps our thinking needs to be transformed regarding these worldly shells we call bodies. May we comfort each other with these words of Paul: "The dead will be raised imperishable, and we will be changed. For the perishable must clothe itself with the imperishable, and the mortal with immortality. When the perishable has been clothed with the imperishable, and the mortal with immortality, then the saying that is written will come true: 'Death has been swallowed up in victory. Where, O death, is your victory? Where, O death, is your sting?'" (1 Corinthians 15:52-55).

• Many people fear death, but it is something believers should never fear. Paul makes it seem as natural and easy as falling asleep, and the Old Testament tells us: "There is a time for everything...a time to be born and a time to die" (Ecclesiastes 3:1-2).

• May even our death bring glory to God, for Jesus once shared with Peter – "the kind of death by which Peter would glorify God" (John 21:19).

Jim was a mighty man of God and he glorified God with his life in ways too numerous to count. But it's very possible that he glorified God in even greater ways through his dying. Jim is one of my heroes.

Heart check: Here are important questions to ponder...

What if whatever you're praying and hoping for doesn't happen? Is God still good? Will you allow the enemy forces of disbelief, fear, and doubt to invade and take over?

8

$\backsim$

Complacency is Deadly

*I*n her book, *On the edge: Leadership Lessons from Mount Everest and Other Extreme Environments,* Alison Levine gives leadership lessons learned through her experiences in mountaineering and polar exploration. She has climbed the highest peak on each continent, skied to both the North and South Poles, and skied a 600-mile remote route across Antarctica as part of a five-person international team. She has survived in some of the most extreme environments known to man.

Summit attempts gone bad

In her writing, Levine relays some riveting stories of summit endeavors gone bad (although most of them were successful). In 1982, one of the best female climbers in the world, Marty Hoey, plunged to her death as she attempted to scale Mount Everest on the peak's north side. At only 31, she was aspiring to be the first American woman to summit Everest. Her training and experience were extensive. She had been a guide for 13 years and had successfully summitted Mount Rainier more than 100 times. She had vast experience on big peaks, with successful climbs of Peak Lenin (23,406 feet) in the former Soviet Union and Nanda Devi (25,634 feet) in India. Levine describes what happened.

After her death, her climbing partners concluded that she had not fastened her harness buckle correctly, as the harness was still attached to the rope when she fell 6000 feet down the Great Couloir on the north side of Everest. The climbers were at 26,600 feet of elevation at the time, where the frigid temperatures make dexterity a challenge and the lack of oxygen makes it hard to think clearly. Marty's accident occurred because she had failed to rethread the end of the waist belt back through the harness buckle (known as "double-backing"). The tragedy is that this fatal error was so avoidable.[A]

She recounts another tragedy that occurred along the same vein to one of the world's best rock climbers, Todd Skinner. He died as he descended along a route on Leaning Tower in Yosemite National Park in California in 2006.

Skinner died when the belay loop on his harness broke. A belay loop is a piece of webbing that connects the waist belt to the leg loops, and it is also where the carabiner is attached for belaying or rappelling. At some point prior to that climbing trip, Skinner had realized his belay loop was worn and had ordered a new harness, but it had not yet arrived. So he continued to climb using the old harness... Harnesses are neither expensive nor difficult to find. They're easy to replace. But it's also easy to say, 'Oh, it'll be fine for *one more climb*.' Sadly, Todd didn't get one more climb."[B]

A deadly way to live

Levine reminds us that "Some of the world's most talented climbers have lost their lives because they let down their guard—they got a little complacent—when things seemed to be under control."[C] We are all vulnerable and can't afford to compromise in even the smallest of details. "Complacency," she says, "will kill you."[D]

> The complacency of fools
> will destroy them.
> Proverbs 1:32b

By being careless with their preparation and putting themselves at risk, these climbers jeopardized not only their lives, but also the safety of other climbers who would spend unnecessary time and take needless risks on treacherous terrain trying to rescue them or retrieve their corpses. No one's climb is solitary. Every climber's experience impacts the lives of other climbers in some manner, positive or negative.

Repeatedly taking risks because you've gotten away with it before or letting certain disciplines slide are dangerous forms of complacency.

Experienced mountain climbers expect the landscape to constantly change. Jet streams can blow in at a moment's notice with sudden wind speeds reaching upwards of 175 miles per hour. Massive ice towers, called *seracs*, are always moving. If the sun comes out and softens the ice, these monstrous, building-size ice chunks may collapse onto the route, either crushing climbers or totally blocking their path and demolishing their trek to the summit.[E] It is essential that the climbers remain in a state of readiness to react to whatever changes come about.

Further consequences of complacency

Pastor Kyle Mercer recounted a fascinating study during one of his sermons. The late Howard Hendricks of Dallas Theological Seminary conducted a study of 246 Christian leaders who had experienced a moral failure. By all accounts, these men were born-again followers of Jesus. So what happened? How did they fall into sin so profoundly? The study disclosed that every one of those Christian leaders admitted they had all but ceased having a daily time of prayer and Bible reading. And each of the men, without exception, knew that this sort of thing "would never happen to me."[F]

Mercer states, "Somewhere along the line, they stopped walking with the Lord."[G] These Christian leaders became complacent about their devotional life. What a perfect inroad for the enemy who will take advantage of such opportunities every single time. He is adept at tempting us to fail when our guard is down.

Malachi, a prophet in Jerusalem, lived about 2450 years ago. He was very disturbed to see how lazy the priests had become in their devotion to God. They had grown lax in their religious behavior and disciplines, causing others to backslide. He warned the priests to live a life of reverence for God as Levi, the very first priest, did. Levi, he reminded them, "walked with [the Lord] in peace and uprightness"[1] and stayed blameless. Levi didn't experience moral failure because he didn't become complacent in his faith; instead, he sought the Lord completely.

Wise Christians know that things never stay the same. We all are climbing some mountain every day. And we expect the landscape of our lives to constantly change. Ice shifts will occur, catching us off guard. Temptations blow in at a moment's notice and pose a myriad of expressions.

We know it is essential that we remain in a state of readiness to react to whatever temptations arise. Otherwise the enemy will pull us down in no time flat! Satan knows that God will never do anything to hurt His relationship with us. Consequently, Satan sends temptations our way, knowing that if we compromise, we will be at risk of falling. Our compromise will also negatively impact the lives of others, leaving them vulnerable, as no one's climb is solitary. And sadly, we risk harming our relationship with God.

Be aware and don't let this happen. Be prepared. Don't let your guard down and allow complacency to define you. It's a dangerous spot to be.

---

[1] Malachi 2:6b

9

Overcoming Complacency

A powerful story is told in Revelation. Jesus instructs John to write to the seven churches in Asia Minor. In this passage, He zeroes in on the church in Laodicea, now western Turkey. It thrived for centuries. Resting on the hills south of the Lycus River valley, Laodicea was considered the greatest city in the area. The population likely reached over 150,000. It was the boom town in the Roman period with giant bathhouses, a large theater, and a stadium. It boasted three major flourishing industries which fueled economic prosperity. The banking industry was thriving. The textile industry was known for its vibrant production of an unusual glossy black wool which was in high demand. A notable medical school was famous far and wide for an eye salve which cleared up infection.[A] The church had grown self-sufficient and had become complacent in their faith, pursuing worldly wealth, fame, and success rather than the internal riches of a God-centered life. Jesus had not one positive thing to say about this church—not one!

Despite its many attributes, this city had always had issues with its water supply. At one time, it had no water source, so a 6-mile-long aqueduct was built to carry hot water from the north, Hierapolis Hot Springs. The water was too far from the source, so by the time it reached the city, it was "lukewarm with a gritty concentration of calcium carbonate."[A]

Colossae was located to the south and was known for refreshing cold mountain run-off. An aqueduct piped this cold water eleven miles to Laodicea, but by the time it reached its destination, it too was lukewarm.[B]

We know that hot water is comforting, and cool water is refreshing, but lukewarm water is mostly useless. Additionally, this lukewarm water was a perfect medium for germs. Hot water kills germs and cold water inhibits the growth of germs, but lukewarm water is a cesspool for bacterial growth. The water functioned as an emetic, causing some to vomit because they became sick with the bacteria this water harbored. God reprimanded this church for their complacent, lukewarm faith due to their feelings of self-sufficiency:

> I know your deeds, that you are neither cold nor hot.
> I wish you were either one or the other!
> So, because you are lukewarm
> —neither hot nor cold—
> I am about to spit you out of my mouth.
> Revelation 3:15-16

Some Christians make God weep; some make him angry. But the self-righteous church at Laodicea just made Him sick. The Greek word in this passage for *spit* actually means "vomit with force."

Lukewarm Christians are not on fire for God; instead they have drifted off the mark and have become complacent, yet what is most tragic is that most don't even realize it. Complacency is spiritually crippling. The Laodiceans thought they were good to go. They had achieved mighty things, fulfilled all their dreams, and were basking in their accomplishments. God had entrusted them with wealth so they could bless others, but they failed! They weren't being good stewards of this wealth. The more self-sufficient they became, the more they shut God out of their lives. They had lost their focus. They had grown complacent, apathetic, and oh-so-comfortable such that they neglected serving God sacrificially. They were too busy enjoying the pleasures of the world and had become indifferent toward their own spiritual poverty. They were living for themselves, not for God, and certainly not for serving others with God's love. This made God sick.

This church had the wrong temperature—lukewarm—not good for much of anything. Jesus uses language this church would understand. Hot vs. cold vs. lukewarm was a clear word picture that would have made perfect sense to them because of their ongoing water supply problem.

A nonbeliever is easier to reach than someone who thinks he is saved but is living outside of God's will without regrets or repentance.

We have much to learn from the Laodiceans.

Disciplined living

It's important to live with self-discipline and purpose, focusing on several areas in order to avoid a lukewarm faith:

1. **Value and protect your daily quiet time with the Lord.**

    Have you become too busy to read your Bible? Have you forgotten to pray? Has your daily quiet time with the Lord slipped to the back burner? Satan injects busyness, boredom, or distractions to disrupt and destroy this important spiritual discipline.

Without a strong daily grounding to begin our day, our flesh is weakened, and we are likely to ease right into the enemy's hands. As with the mountain climbers, climate changes can catch us by surprise and threaten our climb. Moses warns us,

> Sin is crouching at your door.
> Genesis 4:7b

What powerful imagery! Sin is like a lion, poised and ready to catch you off guard so he can pounce for the kill.

2. **Maintain an awareness of your tendency to drift off the mark.**

   The tendency to drift from focused adherence to our faith is real. Once we get comfortable, it's tempting to become a bit complacent and unguarded. We may coast with regards to our protective gear—our armor of God.[1] We may think, "Good enough is good enough." Drifting in our faith always starts out small and picks up speed the more we get off track, usually without realizing it.

3. **Keep a realistic perspective of sin: its temptation and its destruction.**

   Never forget that we are sinners by nature and not immune to sin's charms. Satan seeks to steal, kill, and destroy[2] by tempting us to make sinful choices. He wants to destroy our careers, our relationships, our joy, our peace, our integrity, and most of all, our relationship with Holy God.

Don't flirt with sin. The skilled and wise mountaineer heeds the warning signs; he knows when to turn around and sacrifice the summit. If a blizzard rolls in, the climbers know they shouldn't push forward, thinking, "I can handle this." This kind of pride can easily lead to their downfall. Wise climbers know and respect their limits.

Likewise, if a temptation blows in, assaulting their weaknesses, wise Christians won't entertain whether they can handle it or not. They heed the warning signs and know their limits; they confidently and decisively turn around and head in the opposite direction.

4. **Purposely choose to walk with the Lord, obeying His Word.**

Adam and Eve were walking daily with God in paradise until the serpent slithered in and led them to sin. Their beautiful union was broken, and Adam and Eve found themselves hiding from God instead of walking with Him as they'd always done.

The Bible praises at least two men whose walk with God was exemplary. Enoch didn't have to experience death; he was taken immediately into heaven. He appears in the Hall of Faith.[3] (Hebrews 11 is often called the "Hall of Faith" chapter of the Bible because it boasts an impressive list of heroes who stood strong on their faith when it was difficult. This is a chapter to encourage us.)

> Enoch walked faithfully with God;
> then he was no more,
> Genesis 5:24

Noah was praised highly by God and he also appears in the Hall of Faith.[4]

> Noah was a righteous man,
> blameless among the people of his time,
> and he walked faithfully with God.
> Genesis 6:9

5. Find a way to serve

Serving others with the love of God is a sure-fire way to ignite our faith. Our climb is never solitary; God blesses us for sharing our gifts and spiritual insights with others.

Living with godly intention

In what ways have you become complacent in your walk with God? Have you given up your routine of Sunday worship (it's my only free day, after all…)? This is a warning sign that you are vulnerable to sin. (By the way, no one falls into sin. One chooses to step into sin of one's own accord.) Are you compromising in areas you know you shouldn't?

No one's sin is solitary (just like no one's climb is solitary). Every person's sin impacts the lives of people around them. Let's simplify this as best we can. After all, God's rules for living are not at all complicated. What does He expect from us? He makes it very clear.

> And what does the LORD require of you?
> To act justly and to love mercy
> and to walk humbly with your God.
> Micah 6:8

It sounds easy, but it's not. It will take strict self-discipline to prioritize your relationship with God and to choose to walk obediently with Him every single day. You must fight complacency with everything you've got. Stay alert. Never think, "That will never happen to me." Don't let your guard down. Realize you're only human and as such, you have weaknesses and vulnerabilities. Rely on God's strength to stay on top of your game.

You may never ski across the icy and unforgiving terrain of Antarctica, nor summit the rugged and foreboding wonders of Mount Everest. But you invariably will face challenges almost as daunting. Life isn't all about living on the mountaintop. It requires dogged determination, attention to detail, awareness of sin, and plenty of self-discipline to summit your personal mountains. The efforts you put into living with intention and care will reap great rewards.

Climb on!

---

[1] Ephesians 6:10-17
[2] John 10:10a
[3] Hebrews 11:5
[4] Hebrews 11:7

10

~∽~

This is Your Life

I set down a large jar and looked out into the sea of expectant faces. "This jar," I said, "represents your life. The inside of the jar represents the time you have available to you. You can see the jar has distinct, solid edges—margins—that show us our time is limited. It's not flexible; it's not endless. We have exactly 24 hours each day. Whatever you put inside your jar will define your life."

I started pouring in some sand. "Sometimes we fill our life with too much menial stuff—things that just don't matter. Things like surfing the internet, checking our Twitter feed, scrolling through Facebook. Maybe perusing Pinterest or Etsy. Perhaps replaying over and over things that people said that made us mad. Or checking frequent pings from our social media apps. Maybe spending too much time with people who aren't good for us. These things don't add value to our lives. They are mindless activities that steal our time."

Next, I started dropping in pebbles. "Then we tend to fill in the gaps with things that matter a little but aren't super important. These things will have some consequences if we don't do them, but the consequences are manageable. Things like clearing out emails or making phone calls, engaging in hobbies, and mowing the lawn."

Then I tried to fit in some big rocks. The challenge I faced to make them fit was obvious. "Now we finally get around to the big things and sadly, we find we have run out of time. We just can't fit them in," I say with exasperation, obviously struggling. "We find ourselves saying things like: 'I'm sorry I didn't make the deadline, but I ran out of time.' Or 'I meant to get that mammogram.' Or 'I never have time to read my Bible.' Or 'I'm always late for work.' Or 'I am sorry, Dad, I missed your birthday, but it's been crazy!' You may hear your spouse saying, 'You never have time for the children.' The big rocks represent the most important things in our life—things that can have serious negative consequences if neglected."

Another Jar

I pulled out an identical large jar. "Here is another scenario," I say. "You can see by looking at this jar, that we have an identical amount of time available to us." I started placing the large rocks into the jar first. "It is always best if we tackle these items first. These are the most important things—things that money can't buy—things like time with our family, going to church, daily time with the Lord, attending our child's games and events, maintaining our health, doctor appointments, exercise, career/job, pursuing our dreams/goals, serving, doing things we love. These are things that, if everything else was lost and only these things remained, our life would still hold meaning and joy. Getting eight hours of sleep at night is also a big rock. This will improve our health and make us more efficient and able to think more clearly."

Then I started tossing in the pebbles. "Once we have our priorities straight, we can add in the things that matter, but not super much. These things do have value and need to get done, but they aren't our very top priorities in life— things like cleaning the house and washing the car, answering emails, fixing that broken lamp, paying bills, running errands, and pursuing hobbies."

I began pouring in the sand. It flowed down the sides and in between the big rocks and pebbles, filling all the small spaces until the jar was completely full. "With your leftover time, you can do things like play video games, peruse Instagram, watch Netflix, or do menial activities—things that just don't matter in the big scheme of things."

Conclusion

"Do you tend to get distracted," I challenged, "by the little things in life? It can happen so easily. By filling your precious time with trivial or unimportant activities, you will run out of time for the things that really matter to you."

"You can see," I continued, "if you don't prioritize the big things first, they'll never fit in. What are your big rocks? These are the things that define you—that give your life purpose and meaning. Unless our big rocks get first priority, the lesser priorities will quickly pour in and devour our time, leaving no room for what's most important. Allowing this to happen robs our lives of value," I say with emphasis.

"But when you zero in on the important things first, you will find you will have more time to fit in the things that need to get done but aren't urgent. You will be amazed at what you can accomplish. And you will have a more peaceful countenance and more joy in the process. And perhaps, if time permits, you can add in those things that are mindless, but fun. You can play a couple games of Solitaire or Words with Friends. You can surf the internet or get lost on social media. You'll be surprised to see that when living this way, things have a way of working out."

This activity brought a collective contemplative silence. Time—our most valuable commodity. None of us know how many days we have been given. Let's be good stewards of our time and use our hours wisely as this glorifies God.

> Teach us to realize the brevity of life,
> so that we may grow in wisdom.
> Psalm 90:12 (NLT)

An Exercise

Over the next week, make a list of all the things you are involved in. List your obligations to your family, your friends, your career. Itemize your hobbies, dreams, aspirations, and responsibilities. Record all the ways you spend your time. If you are married, do this with your spouse. Then decide what are your big rocks, what are your pebbles, and what is your sand. (I'd like to suggest some big rocks. It's important to take the time to update your will, make your living will, designate guardians for your children should you and your spouse suffer an accident together, and appoint your power of attorneys for healthcare/finances.)

By setting your priorities and making a strategic plan for your days, you won't find yourselves at the end of your lives, filled with regret at never having accomplished your dreams or prioritizing the most meaningful goals in your life. Instead, you will feel much more in control, be more productive, experience more satisfaction, and find that you seem to have so much more time to fit everything in. Your life will have significantly more meaning.

The rest is just sand.

Disclaimer

This is a common exercise in time management. It has been used so many times that I do not know the original source. But it paints a powerful picture.

11

~~

Run Toward Victory!

*I*t was a most unusual battle! Peculiar, some would say. It took place not between armies, but between two of the most unlikely people. It may be the most well-known battle in the Old Testament. We tell the story to our children. We teach it in Sunday School. Likely you know it well. It's the story of David and Goliath.

The year was about 1020 BC. For nearly 200 years, the Philistines harassed and oppressed the Israelites. The Israelites were terrified of them and couldn't compete with their impressive military might. The Philistines had the most powerful and advanced technology in the world at that time. They incorporated iron into their weapons and tools, something other countries didn't yet have the ability to do. They were a formidable opponent and things had come to a head.

The two nations were in a major standoff. King Saul and the Israelites gathered daily on one hill and the Philistines on another hill with a vast valley between them. The Philistines boasted their champion; Goliath was a fierce and savage warrior standing about 9 feet, 9 inches tall! Huge by today's standards, he would have been absolutely massive in biblical times. He sported an impressive coat of armor from head to ankles, weighing about 125 pounds; his spearhead alone weighed about 15 pounds.[A] He taunted the Israelite army every morning and evening for 40 days, challenging them to select a man to fight him. Saul and his army were paralyzed by fear.

During this time, David (the youngest in a family of eight boys) was working as a shepherd. He was likely a teenager, perhaps between the ages of 12 and 15. One day, his father sent David with roasted grain, bread, and cheese to the army of which his three oldest brothers were a part. David was stunned to watch the deplorable scene unfold before him. He was disgusted with the arrogance and cockiness of this big bully. David was undaunted by Goliath's threats and greatly disturbed that he dare "defy the armies of the living God."[1] David stood strong in faith and remembered previous victories when he killed a lion or a bear which had carried off a sheep from the flock.[2] His heart broke for God's people and swelled with courage to defend God's honor.

David demonstrated remarkable strength of character. When he voiced his intention to go forward and fight Goliath on behalf of the Israelite army, his oldest brother was quick to criticize and mock him. Yet David set his sights on the battle ahead. He refused to be intimidated. He was not to be deterred. He chose his weapon, a sling and five smooth stones, opting for the weapon he knew best. This is what he used when defending his flock.

Goliath despised David and cursed him. Just before their battle, Goliath spoke these words to David:

Come here…
and I'll give your flesh
to the birds and the wild animals!
1 Samuel 17:44

Strengthened by his faith, David replied,

> You come against me with sword
> and spear and javelin,
> but I come against you in
> the name of the LORD Almighty,
> the God of the armies of Israel,
> whom you have defied...
> the battle is the LORD's,
> and he will give all of you
> into our hands.
> 1 Samuel 17:45, 47b

Then "David ran quickly toward the battle line" to attack this giant in his life.[3] And he didn't take on this enemy alone; he came in the name of the Living God, equipped with only five smooth stones.

In the hands of a capable shepherd, a stone can be thrown at speeds up to 100 mph. Archaeologist John Reid notes, "The biggest sling stones are very powerful — they could literally take off the top of your head."[B] And so it happened with David as he met forces with Goliath. He killed him quickly with one carefully aimed stone. A victorious David stood above a dead Goliath—an enormous foe! (Please read the full story in 1 Samuel 17.)

Your battle

Whether you realize it or not, my friends, you are in the front lines of THE battle...the most important battle you will ever face...the battle for your very soul. We all face a Goliath, but only one; that Goliath is Satan. And He will place many *giants* in our lives to try to bring us down, distract us, and make us ineffective for the Kingdom. Yet, be assured that if we are believers, we do not fight alone. Our Lord walks ahead of us, leading the way into battle. And He carries us through.

The more we stand for God, the more the enemy will storm and thrash about, seeking our destruction. He knows what it will take to turn our eyes off God. But if we stand strong for God and His Kingdom, if we step out in confidence to do God's will, if we refuse to water down the gospel and the reason for the hope we have, the more threatened he becomes. And he won't rest. He won't let it go.

Goliath didn't hide the fact that he sought to destroy Israel. In the same way, Satan seeks our destruction, simply because we represent God.

> Be alert and of sober mind.
> Your enemy the devil prowls around
> like a roaring lion looking
> for someone to devour.
> 1 Peter 5:8

Our Goliath, Satan, yells his threats and insults at us day and night. Perhaps he threatens you with anxiety or worry. Maybe depression or doubt. Perhaps for some of you, he uses addictions or obsessions. For many of you, fear is paralyzing and won't give up. Or maybe he knows he can threaten your self-esteem and make you ineffective through thoughts of unworthiness and self-defeat. Or quite possibly, he has placed one or more challenging people in your life who try your patience continually. It's important, in this case, to remember that these people are not your enemies; Satan is. He simply uses them as pawns to bring you down and weaken your defenses.

Our struggle is not against flesh and blood,
but against the rulers, against the authorities,
against the powers of this dark world
and against the spiritual forces
of evil in the heavenly realms.
Ephesians 6:12

Satan is unrelenting and he uses very specific weaponry against each one of us. To fight effectively, we must:

put on the full armor of God,
so that you can take your stand
against the devil's schemes.
Ephesians 6:11
(Keep reading through verse 18.)

For more details on the armor of God, please read chapter 40.

Are you weary? Are you feeling defeated? Perhaps small and insignificant? Do you feel like you can't persevere? Don't give Satan the satisfaction of seeing you flounder. No matter how enormous your enemy, when God is with you, you stand mighty and strong in the Lord! You can do this. You have nothing to fear. "Nothing will be impossible with God."[4] Stay the course, rely on God, trust Him completely, and He will see you through—victorious! For His glory!

---

[1] 1 Samuel 17:26b
[2] 1 Samuel 17: 34-35
[3] 1 Samuel 17:48b
[4] Luke 1:37, ESV

12

❦

The Salmon Run

Our family went on an Alaskan cruise not long ago. Our ship stopped in Ketchikan—the salmon capital of the world. We were fortunate to be there in August during the annual salmon run. What an incredible treat to witness this spectacular scene! Every year, salmon migrate from the ocean and swim with great determination to the upper reaches of rivers where they spawn on gravel beds. They migrate by instinct. Nothing can stop them. Nothing gets in their way.

Salmon face tremendous odds to accomplish their goal. We watched thousands of salmon—probably tens of thousands—as they fought their way up raging rivers. It takes tremendous energy to keep up the physical rigors of their journey. They need strong swimming and leaping abilities to battle the rapids and other obstacles they will face. Some jump up small waterfalls and turbulent rapids by leaping out of the water in hopes of reaching higher ground. Atlantic Salmon have been recorded making vertical jumps almost as high as twelve feet in the air in order to rise above and get past obstacles.[A] What a fascinating marvel.

Just watching the salmon completely exhausted me. I found myself not-so-secretly cheering on the poor things, wanting them to succeed in their quest! The average journey against strong currents and rapids is 150 miles, but some will travel over 900 miles. And they climb a great distance; some climb nearly 7000 feet (5280 feet = 1 mile) on their trek.[B]

The salmon are so focused on their goal that they do not eat the entire time. And they face daunting threats to their lives.

- Dams can trap them in areas where they can't escape.
- Rapids slamming them against rocks can kill them.
- Predators such as bears, bald eagles, harbor seals, sea lions, birds, otters, and fishermen plot and wait for them as they race north.[C,D]
- Environmental factors such as pollution and climate change pose additional dangers.[E]

When the salmon arrive at their destination, the female will lay a few thousand eggs in a hole in a gravel bed and the male will fertilize the eggs. This is the salmon's innate goal: to spawn and lay the foundation for the next generation. When they accomplish this—their life purpose—they die.

Let me ask a couple of questions

1. How many of you feel like a salmon swimming upstream?
2. Do you sometimes feel like you're in an all-out race in pursuit of a virtually impossible goal which takes every ounce of strength you have?

If I asked you to tell me your life goal, you will likely give me various answers of the same theme. Keep in mind that the goal of the Christian life should be totally different from the goal of a nonbeliever's life. You may describe your goal as striving for heaven. Or being happy. Or helping people. Or pursuing holiness or righteousness. Paul tells us that God's goal for us is to be conformed to the likeness of Jesus.[1] He also tells us that His goal for us is to be holy and blameless.[2]

And I will assure you that if we are Christians, it will be a fight for our lives because *everything* in our world runs counter to these goals. Everything!

If you want to be like Jesus or if you are seeking to be holy, righteous, or blameless, you have a dangerous enemy—one who watches your every move and looks to devour and destroy you at every opportunity.[3] Just like the bear who waits for the salmon to jump at the wrong time, your enemy is waiting for you to make the wrong move so he can bring you down.

As you swim upstream, you will encounter many challenges just as hard as battling the rapids or jumping over waterfalls. You will encounter obstacles that threaten to trap you. You will battle constantly against the culture that will forcibly try to throw you in the opposite direction. The culture will give you various feel-good pieces of advice. They will tell you to "go with the flow." "Quit working so hard." "Let it go." "Why stress it?" People may get even more direct and hurtful with comments as they don't understand what drives you. But that's okay because we strive to please God over man.[4]

You see, as I stood on that bridge watching the salmon, I was mesmerized! I didn't understand why they were driven so fiercely to battle the raging currents. The salmon were intensely motivated beyond anything I'd ever seen. I admired their ambitions, their unwavering focus, their solid determination, their total disregard for what anyone watching from that bridge thought of them. Nothing can stop the salmon as they press on!

As I pondered the salmon, I realized they are driven to reach their goal by instinct—it's their very nature. They don't understand it. They just do it, leaning on their physical abilities to accomplish what they know they need to do.

Swimming for our lives

Think of life as a river. We are all swimming. But rivers aren't swimming pools. They move. They have a current. Sometimes the current is calm; sometimes it is swift. With high rains, the water can become a raging river. Some seasons of our lives are relatively calm and quiet. Other seasons are chaotic and fierce, challenging every resource we have.

As we swim for our lives, we can choose:

- to go downstream with the culture (and be like the world) or
- to go upstream—counterculture—to swim against the current—which means we will face waterfalls, raging rapids, obstacles, and predators. It doesn't sound fun, does it?

Only dead fish go with the flow all the time. Dead fish don't care and are content to drift with the surrounding tide.

We, however, are alive in Christ.[5] I hope we will choose to follow our divine nature and swim upstream. Why? Because that's what we are created to do.

But you see, there is one big difference between our journey and that of the salmon. We aren't driven by instinct; we are driven by the One who lives within us—the Holy Spirit. God doesn't leave us in the river to flounder around on our own, flopping wildly about without purpose, as predators stalk us. It is not His intent to watch us thrashing about as the waves of life repeatedly hammer us, thrusting us into river boulders, drawing us into eddies, and catching us in undercurrents too powerful to navigate in our own strength. As we seek Him, God equips us with the strength and resolve to hold our ground, to keep us composed and confident in order to accomplish His purposes.

Spiritual food

We can't be like the salmon, however, and not eat if we want to be triumphant. I'm talking about spiritual food (daily prayer and Bible reading). Without it, we will become too weak to battle well spiritually and we will default to battling in our own strength; this results in making costly mistakes.

If we aren't nourishing ourselves with God's Word and prayer, we will succumb to exhaustion which manifests itself as discouragement, depression, defeat, poor decisions, and despair. These distract us and make us easy prey for spiritual forces waiting to snatch us out of the river to bring us down—like the bears and bald eagles do with the salmon.

However, if we rely on God's strength, His wisdom, and His direction, we will be victorious. We cannot compromise. We must pursue Jesus—righteousness, holiness, and blamelessness—at all costs. As the strong currents and rapids threaten and distract us, God gives us the grace we need to persevere.[6]

Press on

Sometimes the journey through life's stresses seems so long, but God reminds us it won't last very long. And we can't worry what people think as they watch us. We just need to fix our gaze on the important—the things that cannot be seen by the world—because these are the things that will last forever.

Like me standing on the bridge, shaking my head as I watched the salmon, the world will not understand the way we are unwavering in our determination to battle against the current. They may laugh at us. They may shake their heads, roll their eyes, and think we're crazy. They may even try to stop us. Ignore them. It matters not what anyone thinks. Press on. God is with us and will carry us.

Strategic positioning

Let's look at another important lesson the salmon teach us. The salmon live in the river with all kinds of aquatic life. But when facing battles, they are surrounded on all sides by other salmon. They face the threats together, drawing strength from one another.

Like the salmon, we should never isolate ourselves. We should do life among all kinds of people, but when facing challenges, we go to our tribe—our people—Christians we trust. We must seek their counsel and lean into them for support and encouragement.[7,8]

1. In what ways are you swimming downstream?
   a. The enemy and the culture will always tempt you to go with the flow.
   b. This path leads to destruction.

2. In what ways are you swimming upstream—against
    the current?
    a. This is exhausting! It's filled with challenges,
        but worth it.
    b. This path leads to fulfillment because you
        are doing what you were created to do.

As you face the long and tortuous journey ahead, may
the Lord transform you and strengthen you so that you
aren't tempted to go with the dangerous cultural flow of the
world. May He provide Christian friends to help guide and
support you so you aren't victims of the enemy of your soul.
The salmon provide a powerful lesson for us as we seek to
become more like Jesus. It's worth any price you have to
pay as you grow in holiness, giving all glory to the lover of
your soul.

---

[1] 2 Corinthians 3:18a – And we…are being transformed into his
likeness with ever-increasing glory.

[2] Ephesians 1:4 – For He chose us…to be holy and blameless in
his sight.

[3] 1 Peter 5:8 – Be alert and of sober mind. Your enemy the devil
prowls around like a roaring lion looking for someone to
devour.

[4] Acts 5:29b – We must obey God rather than human beings!

[5] 1 Corinthians 15:22b – In Christ all will be made alive.

[6] 2 Corinthians 12:9b – My grace is sufficient for you, for my
power is made perfect in weakness.

[7] Galatians 6:2 – Carry each other's burdens, and in this way you
will fulfill the law of Christ.

[8] 1 Thessalonians 5:11a – Encourage one another and build each
other up.

13

⤫

Two Seas

"You look like someone poured
a bottle of honey on your head!"

*A*nd indeed she was right! My hair was sticking out
in all directions, stiff and unyielding. I had just
emerged from the Dead Sea. My family and I were
touring Israel and had thoroughly enjoyed some time in the
salty waters. I loved it and didn't want to stop floating in
the rich buoyancy. In fact, I was the last one to head to the
showers. Because of my reticence in leaving the water with
the others, I was extremely rushed to get dressed in time to
depart for our next stop—En Gedi.

Although I rinsed my hair, I did a poor job as I had such
limited time. Consequently, I was relegated to looking like
an oddity the rest of the day. But I didn't *really* mind; it was
worth it!

I am a water person. I'm captivated by all things water-
related. And to me, the Dead Sea was an unparalleled
fascination and enigma.

It was May of 2013. When our tour bus pulled up to the
Dead Sea, we all piled out eagerly. Our first observation, as
we approached this massive, unusual body of water was the
striking presence of huge salt crystals covered in sharp,
spiky protrusions; they were everywhere! Even the seabed
was covered with balls of salt crystals; these were smaller,

the size of very large grapes. Walking on them was a painful exercise in stoic torture!

I've gotten ahead of myself. Let's back up a bit...

Two major bodies of water

There are two major bodies of water near where Jesus lived. One is the Sea of Galilee and the other, the Dead Sea.

The Sea of Galilee is a beautiful freshwater lake, thirteen miles long and seven miles wide,[A] sitting 695 feet below sea level. It is only 150 feet deep and is the main water supply for Israel.[B] It is teeming with life! Fish are abundant and foliage in and around the lake is lush and thriving.[A] Israel's largest freshwater lake, the Sea of Galilee, is unquestionably picturesque.

The Dead Sea is also beautiful, but that's where the comparison ends. Looks can be deceiving. The Dead Sea, situated between two mountain ranges, is 31 miles long and 9.3 miles wide. It is a whopping 1237 feet deep[C] and holds the record for the lowest point on Earth at 1410 feet below sea level.[D] Located in a desert, seven million tons of water evaporate from the Dead Sea every day[A] and the water is decreasing by about three feet/year![C] Before the water began dropping, the Dead Sea measured about fifty miles long and eleven miles wide.[D] The Judean Desert only receives an average of about 2.5 inches of rain every year, making it challenging to conserve the water resources.[C]

The Dead Sea lives up to its name because no animals, fish, seaweed, or plants can survive in this particularly toxic environment. If a fish accidentally swims into its waters from one of the freshwater streams that feed it, the fish dies instantly and its body quickly becomes coated with salt crystals.[A]

The Dead Sea is desolate, barren, and lifeless. Only a few microorganisms, algae,[E] and hardy bacteria.[D] can live in this water. The water holds about ten times as much salt as the oceans of the world with a composition of 26-35% salt. This salt concentration acts like an acid.[A] In fact, we were warned not to ingest any of the water as it can be very dangerous—even fatal. And if our hand was in the Dead Sea, we were told not to rub our eyes (like I accidentally managed to do); it sure burns! If I had submerged myself, the salt water would likely have left me blind from permanent burns to my eyes.[F] Divers wear full face masks as protection. If they accidentally swallow this salt water, the larynx can inflate rapidly, resulting in asphyxiation and death.[F]

And yet, a panoramic view of the shores of the Dead Sea left us awestruck with the lavish abundance of huge, sparkling white crystals of salt. There's nothing like it anywhere. What a treasure to behold!

Two bodies of water—yet very different

Although both the Sea of Galilee and the Dead Sea are fed by the Jordan River, one important distinction exists. The Jordan River flows into the Sea of Galilee from the north. The water passes through, then funnels back into the river to the south.[C] This sea has an outlet. It acts like a conduit (or a channel) through which the water travels. As a result, the Sea of Galilee is full of vibrant life and exceptional beauty.

The Dead Sea, on the other hand, only takes water from the Jordan River; it doesn't pass through. Without an outlet, this sea gives no water back.[C] It acts like a container; the water is trapped in the sea and only evaporates, increasing the concentration of the salt and minerals. The salt can only crystallize. The water becomes stagnant, acidic, and void of life.

It takes no effort to float in this *very* warm water; it's like bath water. With minimal effort, my legs just drifted up naturally. As I lazily floated in the Dead Sea on this beautiful, clear day, gazing in rapt wonder at the crystallized shore against a picturesque backdrop of the desolate mountains of Israel and Jordan as they encircled us, I had a lot to ponder.

The life of a Christian

As Christians, we have two options: we can be like the Sea of Galilee or like the Dead Sea. We all take in; it's easy to receive. On Sundays, we enjoy the worship service, we digest a good sermon, we partake of the benefits of our church membership with its various programs. But here's the rub; do we give back? Are we a conduit or a container?

Jesus set the example. He is referred to as "the spring of living water"[1] All of us thirst. We experience both physical thirst and spiritual thirst. As physical water hydrates the body's organs and is essential for survival, spiritual water is essential for eternal survival as it restores the soul. Many of us are spiritually dying of thirst.

> As the deer pants for streams of water,
> so my soul pants for you, my God.
> My soul thirsts for God, for the living God.
> Psalm 42:1-2a

Are you thirsty? Do you long for a life-giving spring of cool, refreshing water?

Jesus is offering living water.[2] He tells us that as we partake of it, we will become "a spring of water welling up to eternal life"[3] and never thirst again! Living water refers to the Holy Spirit. As we partake in a personal relationship with Jesus, we drink living water as the Holy Spirit indwells us, sealing us for salvation and eternal life.[4]

> "Let anyone who is thirsty, come to me and drink.
> Whoever believes in me…rivers of
> living water will flow from within them."
> By this he meant the Spirit, whom those
> who believed in him were later to receive.
> John 7:37b-39a

Jesus clearly chooses life for us! We must be consuming living water and offering it to others. He tells us, "It is more blessed to give than to receive."[5] As we generously offer the precious living water that we have personally received, we become more vibrant, full of life, and life-giving to others!

If, however, we define our lives as takers only, rather than givers—spiritual intake with no spiritual output—the outcome is radically different. We become self-absorbed, stagnant, acrid, and lifeless—fun for a while, perhaps, but we will end up getting burned.

Conduit or container—life or death—your choice.

---

[1] Jeremiah 17:13

[2] John 4:10

[3] John 4:14

[4] Ephesians 1:13b-14a – When you believed, you were marked in him with a seal, the promised Holy Spirit, who is a deposit guaranteeing our inheritance.

[5] Acts 20:35b

14

Blessed Be the Name of the Lord

The Lord gives, and the Lord takes away.
Blessed be the name of the Lord.
Job 1:21, CSB

The Lord gives us many blessings throughout our lives. The words, *give* and *gift* share the same root. A gift is something entrusted to us without expectation of payment. And blessings from God are just that…gifts. Earthly gifts are transient, not necessarily meant to last forever.

- He gives us grandparents…and He takes them away.
- He gives us parents…and He takes them away.
- He gives us pets…and He takes them away.
- He gives us our career…and He takes it away as we embrace retirement.
- He gives us a comfortable home…and He takes it away as we transition to a nursing home.
- He gives us our health…and He takes it away as we gradually age.
- He gives us money and possessions…and He takes them away at death…left for someone else to enjoy.
- He gives us a body and He takes it away as our body is separated from our soul at death (and we get our glorified body when Christ returns).

- He gives us pleasures…and He takes them away as our memories fade.
- He gives us the seasons…and He takes them away as they slowly but surely meld into the next season.
- He gives us a snowfall…until the sun emerges to melt the pure, powdery splendor.
- He gives us children…and He takes them away to college or careers to make their mark in the world.
- He gives us the beauty and strength of youth…which yield to the aging of the years.

(Please read Ecclesiastes 3:1-8.)

Every single gift in our lives is from the Lord.[1] Sadly though, I can't think of one earthly gift that we can keep for a lifetime. Everything in this chaotic, imperfect world is in constant flux. Nothing stays the same—except for God, His characteristics, and His Word. These are the only constants that never change. In a world that spins in continual turmoil, how comforting it is to embrace the fact that God never changes.

In 1923, Thomas Obediah Chisholm, a Methodist minister, penned the words to a beautiful and popular hymn, *Great is Thy Faithfulness*, inspired by Lamentations 3:22-23.[2] In that hymn is this line, "Thou changest not, thy compassions, they fail not; as thou hast been thou forever wilt be."

God is most generous to shower us with gifts, yet we frequently take them for granted. We often don't appreciate the fact that there will come a time in the future when we will have to live on without them—when we must relinquish those gifts.

78

Shortly before her death, Corrie ten Boom attended Pastor Charles Swindoll's church in Southern California. After chatting about his wife and children, Corrie ten Boom became serious. She reached out her wrinkled hands in front of her, cupping them as if cradling a treasure. In her strong Dutch accent, she shared a poignant piece of advice.

> Pastor Svendahl, you must learn to hold everyting loosely ... everyting. Even your dear family. Why? Because da Fater may vish to take vun of tem back to Himself, und ven He does, it vill hurt you if He must pry your fingers loose.[A]

Just as we receive gifts from our loving Father in submission, with gratitude and open hands, we must be willing to release them back to Him, with gratitude and open hands, and in His perfect timing.

Pastor Swindoll wisely stated,

> Since our Lord is sovereign, not only are our times in His hands, so are all our possessions and all the people we love. Releasing our rights to Him includes the deliberate releasing of our grip on everything and everyone.

Is this easy?
Never.
But it's necessary.

---

[1] James 1:17a – Every good and perfect gift is from above.
[2] Lamentations 3:22b-23 – His compassions never fail. They are new every morning; great is your faithfulness.

15

From Grief to Praise

Why is grieving a loss so painful—so hard? We grieve because we love. Grief is the price we pay for love. The more we love, the more we grieve.

Loss can be sudden or gradual. When sudden, the transition to a new normal can be jolting! When gradual, such as losing a parent to dementia, coping with our worsening health, or moving to a nursing home, the transition can be excruciating. We can feel like we've lost our equilibrium. Life shifts. We feel off kilter. Even good loss (your son or daughter gets married) is still loss. Loss is usually painful, and we mourn.

We wish the gift had lasted longer. We may even be angry. And that's okay! But at some point, we need to turn from inward-focused coping to outward-focused worship as we praise God for the joy we knew as we cherished that gift.

In the wake of all-consuming, devastating loss, Job did not hide his overwhelming heartache and crushing grief. He acknowledged them in deepest sorrow. Yet do you remember the next thing he did?

He chose to praise.

Blessed be the
name of the Lord.
Job 1:21b, CSB

After extensive self-reflection and inward heart-wrenching struggles to come to terms with the disaster his life had become, he chose God. Satan tried to get him to cave, but he courageously chose God. And we can too!

Job shows us how to praise God in our loss and our grief. We praise God because He is worthy of our praise, regardless of our circumstances.[1] We praise God for choosing us to receive and enjoy the gift we have lost. In praising, we turn our focus from our gut-wrenching sorrow to the deep, abiding joy it brought us. We shift from gloom to gratitude. Importantly, we can grieve and praise at the same time.

To hang on too tightly to the things of this world borders on idolatry. Nothing here will last; everything is temporary. We must resist becoming too attached to this world, but instead cast our eyes to our eternal destiny—our everlasting home.

Consider these scenarios:

- Perhaps you lost a dearly loved pet. You quickly find your closest friends cannot understand the depth of this loss because they never owned a pet like yours.
- You now reside in a nursing home, forgotten and lonely. Friends and family have died before you or are busy with other things. The days are long.
- Maybe you lost the most wonderful mother, one to whom you were very close. Yet your best friend doesn't understand your loss because her mother wasn't nurturing or loving like yours.
- Perhaps retirement seems empty and forlorn. Others can't begin to understand that you devoted 40 years in service to a profession you loved. To them, their livelihood was just a job.

- You have been told you will never run again; a disease is robbing you of muscle strength. Friends cannot grasp the magnitude of this loss because being active was never important to them.
- Maybe you buried your son, yet your own sister cannot comprehend the extent of your grief; she never had children.
- A virus damaged your vocal cords; you will never sing again. Friends can't relate; they didn't have vocal talent.

No one can fully appreciate your loss because their experiences will never be the same as yours. That's why loss is so isolating and grief can be so lonely. But Christ understands.

As we grieve our loss, God promises us blessings. Here are several:

- We gain a new perspective as we now see things differently because of our loss.
- Our loss makes us long for the hope of heaven all the more.
- We draw closer to God—where else can we go?
- God extends His comfort and compassion as He understands every emotion we can possibly feel.

If you could choose, would you choose to never have gotten your pet? Would you rather have died at a young age, never experiencing all you did in your lifetime? Would you have preferred a different mother? Would you have chosen a career not nearly as meaningful? Would you opt to have never known the thrill of the race—the joy of victory? Would you choose never to have had a son at all? Would you prefer to never have experienced the pleasure of singing before an audience? I think I know your answers.

It's better to have experienced great joy and now to treasure precious memories of that joy than never to have had the joy at all.

> "What we have once enjoyed
> and deeply loved
> we can never lose,
> for all that we love deeply
> becomes a part of us."
> Helen Keller

When in the throes of grief, especially following a significant loss or tragedy, we may wonder how we will survive. We may be so gripped with the pain of grief that we are certain we cannot go on—like we cannot take another step. We are sure we are breathing our final breath. Our strength is gone as grief overtakes us. We cry out to God in desperation. "God, help! I need to know you see me—that you're here." We often don't even know what to ask for, but the Holy Spirit promises to take over, interceding for us.

> The Spirit also helps our weakness;
> for we do not know
> what to pray for as we should,
> but the Spirit Himself intercedes for us
> with groanings too deep for words.
> Romans 8:26, NASB

When we, like Job, are able to ponder the bigness of God and the smallness of us, He reveals Himself to us. He asks one thing: *trust me.* No matter how painful—how confusing—how much we're suffering, we have one valuable option: to trust the God who rules the universe and loves us with an everlasting love. Amidst all the doubt, fear, anger, and despair, we have one place to lean—on our faith. "God, I choose to trust you. I trust that you see me and I trust that You're here with me."

We may still struggle to make sense of it all. *Why, God?* We think if we can rationalize or reason our way through this, it will be easier. We can't. And it won't. God's ways are so far above our ways.[2] All this will make sense on the other side of heaven when our faith becomes sight. Answers to our questions won't help now; we simply need God.

Nothing is wasted in God's economy. Our suffering isn't for naught. All our suffering and ordeals are producing a harvest more wonderful than words. That is something we can bank on.

Except for very rare cases, it won't always be this hard. The pain will lessen; the tears will be fewer. Time does soften our suffering. We will laugh again and find joy in our days. But first we grieve.

Grief cycles like the tide. When it descends, embrace it. Let it come. Deal with it at your own pace. Do not fight it or rush it. Everyone's journey through grief is different; there is no normal. Your grief is your own. It's valuable and necessary in order to heal.

And as we grieve, we trust—we trust that God is sovereign over all things. We trust He knows what He's doing. He's worthy of our trust—and our praise. When we praise as we grieve, we glorify our Father in heaven.

Heaven

Our final home will be all joy and no loss. We will never have to say good-bye. There will be no more tears. No grief. No letting go. Only laughter—and embracing —and praise! Everything will finally make sense. Death, loss, suffering, sorrow, and tears do *not* have the final word!

Therefore, while we are still here, let's choose to recognize our gifts with gratefulness, enjoy them while we have them, appreciate the gift giver, and be willing to let them go in God's timing. And when they are gone, we can embrace and savor the sweet and cherished memories those gifts have left behind. And let's realize that our time here is short. One day soon, we will be in our eternal home where we may not even remember our tears here on earth. And even if we do, we will be too busy rejoicing to waste time revisiting our earthly losses. They just won't matter any longer.

Praise be to God!

---

1 Psalm 96:4a – Great is the LORD and most worthy of praise.

2 Isaiah 55:9 - As the heavens are higher than the earth, so are my ways higher than your ways and my thoughts than your thoughts.

16

~~

Three Trees and Three Gardens

"A tree gives glory to God by being a tree.
For in being what God means it to be,
it is obeying Him."
Thomas Merton

*T*rees are the oldest living things on earth and are mentioned in the Bible more than any living thing, except for God and people.[A] There are trees in the first chapter of Genesis, the first Psalm, the first book in the New Testament (Matthew) and the last (Revelation).[A] In the King James Bible, there are 287 verses that mention trees. More than 36 different kinds of trees are mentioned throughout scripture.[B]

Trees symbolize life and endurance. Interestingly, during His time on earth, Jesus was a carpenter by trade, working with trees and the wood they provide to bring forth beauty in the items He crafted.

In the Bible, there are three specific trees that hold special importance and interestingly, each tree correlates to a unique garden of divine significance.

The first tree and garden –
The fall of man

Early in Genesis, we see Adam and Eve enjoying a perfect world communing daily with God in perfect fellowship in the pristine Garden of Eden filled with glorious trees. We are introduced to two trees in this garden, one of which is the Tree of the Knowledge of Good and Evil. God gave Adam and Eve total freedom to eat from any tree in the garden except for the Tree of the Knowledge of Good and Evil.[1]

But Adam and Eve yielded to the temptation to sin at the hands of the crafty serpent (Satan); they ate from this tree which yielded two devastating results.

- Spiritual death (separation from God) as they were driven from the garden.
- Physical death (they would now die and be denied access to the second tree in Eden, the Tree of Life).[2] We, too, are separated from the Tree of Life, but not forever.

Symbol of death

The Tree of the Knowledge of Good and Evil and the Garden of Eden tell the story of the fall of mankind into sin. The consequences were devastating as sin and death spread to all men and women who came after them.[3] And all of creation would be subject to decay and death.

The second tree and garden –
The sacrifice for man

The Garden of Gethsemane, located on the Mount of Olives, is the second garden. After the "last supper" that Jesus shared with His disciples, they walked to this garden where Jesus spent a tortuous night in intense, earnest prayer to the Father. It was here that He was betrayed by Judas and arrested by the soldiers, then led away to be unjustly condemned to death.

It was pure evil that chopped down a mighty tree, stripped it of its branches and foliage, and erected it in the ground with a cross piece just outside the city of Jerusalem. This second tree became the cross on which Jesus was crucified.

A living tree was destroyed. On it was placed the Bread of Life. They killed Jesus on that tree instead of us. But in full splendor and glory, Jesus rose to new life. The tree was killed, but it brought forth life everlasting.

Symbol of life

This tree—the cross—is a symbol of the life of Jesus Christ, whose sacrificial act of love made it possible for us to be forgiven for all our sins, restored in fellowship with God, rescued from judgment, and saved for eternity.

The Garden of Gethsemane is known for the place where Jesus retreated alone on His knees in the dark night beneath the shelter of olive trees. It was here that He cried out to His Father in anguish, wrestling in great sorrow with what was before Him. And it was here that He resolutely submitted to the plan to redeem mankind and all of creation from the grip of sin and death to life everlasting.

Suffering comes before deliverance. Anguish comes before peace. The cross comes before the glory.

The third tree and garden –
The eternal salvation for man

The third Garden is the Garden of God.[4] It is here that the Garden of Eden—paradise—will be restored. Everything that was lost in the first garden will be restored in the third garden. God will dwell here with man the way he dwelled with Adam and Eve in the Garden of Eden. Death and sin are defeated.[5,6] The curse is gone.[7] There is no more pain, sorrow, or tears.[5] Access to the Tree of Life is now regained.[8] Eternal life has been secured and freedom reigns supreme.[9]

The third tree is the Tree of Life which is in heaven. Everyone has been separated from the Tree of Life since Eden, the first garden. But because of what happened on the second tree—the cross—we will have access to the third tree by accepting Jesus and His great sacrifice on our behalf. We will have the right to eat of the Tree of Life.[8]

The Tree of Life bears 12 fruits (12 represents authority or perfection), one each month of the year, to sustain eternal life continually. And while we may not fully understand what it means, we are told the leaves are for the healing of the nations.[10]

Symbol of resurrection

The Tree of Life and the Garden of God represent salvation and restoration. Everyone has been separated from the Tree of Life. Soon, those who have put their faith in Jesus Christ will have access to it as we share in His victory over sin and death and enjoy paradise eternally with the Lord of our soul.

Three trees—three gardens. They tell the good news of the gospel.

The fall of man.
The victory of Jesus.
The salvation of the world!

To the glory of God—now and for all eternity. Hallelujah!

1 Genesis 2:16-17 – And the LORD God commanded the man, "You are free to eat from any tree in the garden; but you must not eat from the tree of the knowledge of good and evil, for when you eat from it you will surely die."

2 Genesis 3:22-24 – And the LORD God said, "The man has now become like one of us, knowing good and evil. He must not be allowed to reach out his hand and take also from the tree of life and eat, and live forever." So the LORD God banished him from the Garden of Eden to work the ground from which he had been taken. After he drove the man out, he placed on the east side of the garden of Even cherubim and a flaming sword flashing back and forth to guard the way to the tree of life.

3 Romans 5:12 – Just as sin entered the world through one man, and death through sin, and in this way death came to all people, because all sinned.

4 Revelation 21:1-2a – Then I saw a new heaven and a new earth, for the first heaven and the first earth had passed away, and there was no longer any sea. I saw the Holy City, the new Jerusalem, coming down out of heaven from God.

5 Revelation 21:4a – He will wipe every tear from their eyes. There will be no more death or mourning or crying or pain.

6 Colossians 2:13b-14 (MSG) - All sins forgiven, the slate wiped clean, that old arrest warrant canceled and nailed to Christ's cross.

7 Revelation 22:3a – No longer will there be any curse.

8 Revelation 2:7b – To the one who is victorious, I will give the right to eat from the tree of life, which is in the paradise of God.

9 John 6:40 – Everyone who looks to the Son and believes in him shall have eternal life, and I will raise them up at the last day.

10 Revelation 22:2b – On each side of the river stook the tree of life, bearing twelve crops of fruit, yielding its fruit every month. And the leaves of the tree are for the healing of the nations.

17

~~

Born Twice - Die Once

"If you have been born only once,
you will have to die twice.
But if you have been born twice,
you will have to die only once."[A]
David Jeremiah

*A*ll of us were born into this world from our mother's womb. This is our physical birth. And all of us will die at the end of this life—our physical death. At our death, our soul leaves our body and either enters into God's presence or is forever separated from Him.

Some people have given everything they have to avoid death, but in the end, they have failed. Several hundred people have even paid huge sums of money to have their bodies frozen upon their death to await the invention of a magic potion that will ensure immortality. Let's face it, unless Jesus returns beforehand, we all will face physical death during our lifetime. It is inescapable.

Some of us will experience a second birth. And others of us will endure a second death. Confusing? Let's dive in deeper for clarification.

Second birth

There was a Pharisee named Nicodemus. He was a devoutly religious man, although he wasn't a Christian. He came to see Jesus one night because he was grappling with faith issues, and he wanted to know more. He was convinced Jesus was a teacher of God because he witnessed remarkable miracles that He had performed. Yet Nicodemus didn't believe Jesus was the Son of God...not yet anyway. Nicodemus was most concerned about the afterlife.

As Nicodemus started talking, Jesus immediately zeroed in on the heart of the issue and replied, "No one can see the kingdom of God unless they are born again."[1] Nicodemus furrowed his brow and shook his head; he didn't understand. "Surely they cannot enter a second time into his mother's womb to be born!"[2] Jesus explained that the kingdom is offered to the whole world, but "No one can enter the kingdom of God unless they are born of water and the Spirit...You must be born again."[3] Nicodemus tried so hard to grasp everything Jesus was sharing.

Jesus was making a point that to experience eternal life in the kingdom of heaven, one must be born not only of water (our physical birth), but also of the Spirit (our spiritual birth). People don't enter heaven by living a good life, but by spiritual rebirth; that's the only way.

The Bible tells us that when a person puts his faith in Christ, this is called a spiritual rebirth; he is born again. He is changed eternally by this decision and offered a new life.[4] He will still die physically one day like everyone else, but he will never die a second time (spiritual death); he will spend eternity in heaven.

Jesus said, "I am the resurrection and the life.
He who believes in me will live, even though they die;
and whoever lives by believing in me will never die."
John 11:25-26

Second death

When a person chooses not to place his faith in Jesus Christ, he chooses to rely on himself to get to heaven, which is an impossible feat. When a person stands before holy God on Judgment Day—relying on his own merit—the outcome will be devastating. This person will experience a second death which is a spiritual death—permanent separation from God. Peter warns us that the Lord is terribly grieved when people reject Him. He doesn't want anyone to perish through the second death, but to come to repentance.[5]

John elaborates further to say that sinners who have not repented, and who do not trust Jesus for the forgiveness of their sins, will experience this second death—spiritual death—at God's final judgment. "The unbelieving...will be consigned to the fiery lake of burning sulfur. This is the second death."[6]

What will it be?

Born twice—die once. Or born once—die twice. It's up to you. A wise person once said, "Non-Christians only meet to part again; Christians only part to meet again."

Your eternal destination is your choice. Only those who put their faith in Jesus Christ and are born again will be saved from destruction. Puritan Thomas Watson wrote, "Eternity to the godly is a day that has no sunset. Eternity to the [unsaved] is a night that has no sunrise."

Don't put off this decision. Grapple with it and do like Nicodemus did; go to Jesus with your questions. He will guide you into Truth.

---

[1] John 3:3b
[2] John 3:4b
[3] John 3:5b,7b
[4] Romans 6:4 – We were therefore buried with him through baptism
   into death in order that, just as Christ was raised from the dead
   through the glory of the Father, we too may live a new life.
[5] 2 Peter 3:9
[6] Revelation 21:8

18

‿◦‿

The Ancient Paths

When we are burdened, the world seems a colder place, harsh even. The sun shines, yet we don't notice. Birds sing, but we don't hear them. Flowers bloom, but we can't see them. Friends are available—if only we would remember that. The Lord is with us, but we don't feel His presence. In many ways, we are paralyzed—in limbo. We don't know which way to turn.

Jeremiah would understand. He was a prophet to Judah, the southern kingdom of Israel. He carefully watched the people he cared so much about. He agonized as they screwed up over and over, never heeding his prophetic advice. They acted on their feelings, whims, and passions which changed with the cultural tide. So often, he saw them in despair, at a crossroads, as if traveling down a road and being confused about which direction to turn. They were lost, needing direction, as they often chose the wrong path.

With Jerusalem under siege, God offered this advice.

> *Stand* at the crossroads and *look*;
> *ask* for the ancient paths,
> *ask* where the good way is, and *walk* in it,
> and you will *find rest* for your souls.
> But you said, "We will not walk in it."
> Jeremiah 6:16, emphasis mine

Jeremiah broke down his advice into five parts.

1) Stand

Don't move until you know which direction to go.
There are two sets of paths—two ways to turn. You are
at a crossroads and must choose.

The old paths are the paths Israel's godly
ancestors—the saints of old—have trod many times
before, all throughout history. People like Enoch,
Noah, Abraham, Isaac, Jacob, Joseph, Elijah, David,
Moses, Joshua, and many others. These paths never
change. They're the paths of righteousness and
holiness.

Jesus told His followers,

> I am the way
> and the truth and the life.
> No one comes to the Father
> except through me.
> John 14:6

Jesus *is* these ancient paths—the way of access to
God. He is *the way*. He is *the truth* (based on God's
Word). His paths are the *only* paths that lead to
salvation—eternal happiness—and everlasting life.

The other paths are self-made. These paths have
bought into a watered-down doctrine resulting in a
compromised faith which has grown anemic from
adopting worldly, hollow philosophies. These paths are
lined with the idols of our world. And apostasy.
Choosing these paths is a very serious and dangerous
mistake because they lead to destruction in some form
or another.

2) Look

It was customary in that day to have watchmen posted on high towers or on hills to watch for any potential hostile invasions and to alert the people of impending physical danger with a trumpet sound.

The prophets of the day were also often called watchmen because they were on the lookout in a spiritual sense to warn the people of serious spiritual danger that was lurking.

Jesus is our watchman—our guide. We must look to Him—fix our eyes on Him. All paths lead somewhere. Most paths lead to mistakes and regrets. Only the ancient paths lead to glory, honor, and godliness.

3) Ask

Pray for the correct paths—the paths of old. Ask the Lord for courage to walk these paths because they will be the paths less traveled and frequently more difficult to navigate. Ask because these paths aren't the most obvious, the most trusted, the most easygoing, or the safest.

4) Walk

The paths of righteousness may take you through the valley of suffering or the desert of despair. They may take you to the mountaintops of success or through storms of conflict. There are no guarantees. When you choose these paths of old, remember you don't walk alone. Christ is your watchman, and He guides you one turn at a time. As you walk down the street of suffering or along the trail of tears, listen for His voice and follow Him. Trusting Him in the journey honors Him. Draw on the Spirit's strength; He will carry you.

5) Find rest

When you choose to walk the ancient paths, sweet rest is promised for your soul. It's only when you trust God that you will experience relief from your burdens and peace with God that spill into all areas of your life. The ancient paths are the *only* paths that lead to eternal joy, solid hope, and an unwavering confidence that you are journeying straight to everlasting life—your souls saved from the fire. To experience complete rest in this knowledge and assurance is the most peaceful rest that exists.

Are you at a crossroads, my friend?

Don't just jump in and head down the paths that *seem right* at the time, based on emotions and what others tell you to choose. Don't choose the paths that are the most well-traveled. Stop looking for the paths of least resistance.

Pause and consider your options with eyes wide open. Don't be tempted by the well-worn paths of compromise dictated by a changing cultural tide.

> "Stop looking for the path of
> least resistance and start running
> down the path of greatest glory
> to God and good to others,
> because that's what Jesus,
> the Real Man, did."
> Pastor Mark Driscoll

Ask for the ancient paths founded on the written Word of God—the paths of greatest glory to God. They lead in the way of righteousness and holiness. God hears you call out; He will answer and guide you. Obey His voice and start walking, not looking back, not second guessing your choice.

Then enjoy sweet rest for your soul and peace of mind as you journey through this life in trust and submission, glorifying God with each beautiful step.

What invaluable blessings from the lover of your soul!

19

~<del>⚬</del>~

God Has a Secret

God has a secret. He calls it "the mystery that has been kept hidden for ages and generations."[1] It was hidden throughout the Old Testament and was only revealed in the New Testament. Yet it was not revealed while Jesus was alive; it stayed hidden until He died, was buried, and then resurrected. This "mystery" contained glorious riches and was a blessing like no one ever imagined—like no one could ever fathom. And today it remains just as mysterious, yet more magnificent and wonderful than we can begin to grasp.

> God has chosen to make known…
> the glorious riches of this mystery,
> which is Christ in you,
> the hope of glory.
> Colossians 1:27

The mystery: Christ in you, the hope of glory.

It was part of God's plan from the beginning. He revealed this mystery to the first New Testament believers, about 120 of them, in a rather extraordinary way. Let's peek in and take a look. Those present were His disciples; His mother, Mary; His brothers; and other men and women. Jesus had ascended to heaven ten days earlier.

Fifty days after Jesus's resurrection. Everyone was all together in one place: the Upper Room. (This would have been a very large room in a building, set atop a lower room. Likely this was the same place where the disciples partook of the Last Supper with Jesus, although this cannot be proven irrefutably.) It was here God chose to reveal this glorious mystery—His secret gift—the Holy Spirit.

As these early believers gathered in the Upper Room (remember, this was inside), suddenly the roar of a violent wind thundered from heaven, filling the entire house. The noise was deafening. Their hair and clothing whipped about. Anything on the ground or on a table was blown across the room. The people found it hard to catch their breath in the sudden and intense gusts that ravaged the space.

Everyone froze, shocked, shaken, and probably terrified in wide-eyed wonder at the chaos and turmoil overtaking the room. But this wasn't all; the madness was just starting! Without warning, flaming tongues of fire arose out of nowhere and danced all around and among them. Then the tongues separated and rested on each person in the room. This was a defining moment like no other!

In a dramatic fashion, the Holy Spirit instantly filled each person there! As evidence, everyone started speaking "in other tongues."[2] (Note: this wasn't speaking in spiritual tongues, nor was it gibberish.) They talked in many different known languages that people could understand! What a miraculous, grand display of God's power for this international crowd (people from at least twelve different nations) gathered that day for the Feast of Weeks.

For the first time in history, the unstoppable, uncontainable Holy Spirit came in full power to indwell ordinary men and women.

Jesus gave warnings

Jesus had warned the disciples this would occur, although none of them would have been able to fully grasp the meaning of His words at that time.

> I am going to send
> you what my Father has promised;
> but stay in the city until you have been
> clothed with power from on high.
> Luke 24:49

———

> Do not leave Jerusalem,
> but wait for the gift my Father promised,
> which you have heard me speak about.
> Acts: 1:4b

About 800 years before Jesus was born, Joel prophesied this remarkable outpouring of the Holy Spirit when He said, "I will pour out my Spirit on all people."[3] God's Spirit would now be available to anyone who called on the Lord in faith. He went on to say, "Everyone who calls on the name of the LORD shall be saved."[4] The presence of the indwelling Spirit is our guarantee of this salvation.

Christ in you

The Old Testament is filled with verses that show the Holy Spirit coming upon certain people and staying for a while, empowering them with God's strength to carry out His will. But the Spirit would then leave; it was a temporary empowerment.

During His years of earthly ministry, Jesus walked with His disciples, all aspects of His ministry pointing to the Father. In the flesh, Jesus was finite, and His time here was limited. His life pointed to the gospel wherever he went, but He could only be in one place at a time.

The plan, after His death, was for Him to return in the Person of the Holy Spirit to live inside His followers for the rest of their lives. It was to be a permanent indwelling for New Testament believers. Jesus said, "You will realize that I am in my Father…and I am in you."[5] Let this radical truth penetrate a minute. Can we even begin to process the significance and weightiness of this for us?

As the Spirit indwelt each individual believer with holy power, He was then able to go where each person went, thus aiding in the spread of the gospel worldwide. He could be everywhere and anywhere believers were, pointing to the Father, rather than in the limited space Jesus could occupy at any one time during His incarnation.

When the mystery was revealed and each believer was instantly indwelt by the Holy Spirit, the formal Church was birthed in that Upper Room. These 120 people were the original founders of the Church and the spread of the gospel exploded forth in divine power!

The Holy Spirit

The Holy Spirit is a mighty, unstoppable force available to all those He indwells—believers. The Holy Spirit brings many blessings. Here are some:

- **the Spirit of Truth**
  He guides us into all truth.[6]
- **the Spirit of Promise**
  He promises us eternal salvation as He marks us with a seal—the indwelling Holy Spirit.[7]

- **the Spirit of Wisdom**
  He imparts His divine discernment and wisdom in our lives.[8]
- **the Spirit of Revelation**
  He reveals the person of Jesus Christ to us, aiding us in having a personal relationship with Him.[8]
- **the Spirit of Power**
  He gives us divine ability and energy to carry out God's will.[9]
- **the Spirit of Love**
  He gives us the ability to love supernaturally, impossible in our own strength.[9]
- **the Spirit of a Sound Mind**
  He keeps us grounded and able to discern rationally.[9]
- **the Spirit of Comfort**
  He comforts us in all our afflictions.[10,11]
- **the Spirit of Glory**
  He radiates the glory of Jesus Christ on and through us as we shine with the Light of His presence to a dark world.[12]

The hope of glory

The *hope of glory* is the fulfillment of God's promise to restore us and all of creation.

- ***Hope*** in biblical times carried a radically different meaning than it does to us today. Today it means wishful thinking as in, "I hope that happens." Back then, it meant *a confident expectation of a divine event that would surely occur.*

- **Glory** is a word impossible to adequately define. The best definition I can think of is *divine perfect majesty*. But even this is woefully insufficient.

The Holy Spirit will one day restore all creation, including us, to full glory—back to its divine, perfect condition, like it was in the Garden of Eden, before sin entered in.[13] Christ's presence in us is God's divine mystery—His holy secret—the *hope of glory*.

On to glory

Our ancestors of long ago would refer to the death of someone differently than we do today. They would say, "Uncle Clarence went on to glory." Or "Mrs. Talbott passed on to glory." They meant that someone died and went to heaven in glory—bodies restored to health and wholeness in a paradise of divine perfect majesty.

When my mother was taking her last breaths, I prayed this psalm out loud over her. I did the same for my father-in-law. Both were believers, knew they were never alone, and greatly anticipated heaven. God took them by the hand and guided them into glory.

I am always with you;
you hold me by my right hand.
You guide me with your counsel,
and afterward you will take me into glory.
Whom have I in heaven but you?
And earth has nothing I desire besides you.
My flesh and my heart may fail,
but God is the strength of my heart
and my portion forever.
Psalm 73:23-26

What a beautiful, visual description of a holy reality for Christians. Are you confident that when your days are over, God will take you into glory? You don't have to muddle about, hoping to find your way on your own. Jesus will come for you and carry you there Himself—if you have placed your trust in Him.

The secret revealed

The God of the universe has a secret. It's a secret for those who put their trust in Him. If you don't trust the Creator of the universe, the Creator of all humanity, who are you going to trust? Yourself? Good luck with that. Trust the One living God and receive His mysterious gift—His secret—saved for you—the *hope of glory*. Live in peace—with the hope of glory embedded within your soul. Then one glorious and magnificent day, Jesus will take you on to glory to live with Him forever.

You will never be the same!

---

[1] Colossians 1:26a

[2] Acts 2:4

[3] Joel 2:28a

[4] Joel 2:32a

[5] John 14:20

[6] John 16:13a – When he, the Spirit of truth, comes, he will guide you into all the truth.

[7] Ephesians 1:13b-14 – When you believed, you were marked in him with a seal, the promised Holy Spirit, who is a deposit guaranteeing our inheritance until the redemption of those who are God's possession—to the praise of his glory.

[8] Ephesians 1:17b – the glorious Father may give you the Spirit of wisdom and revelation, so that you may know him better.

9 2 Timothy 1:7 – For God has not given us a spirit of fear, but of power and of love and of a sound mind. NKJV

10 John 14:16 – the Father...shall give you another Comforter, that he may abide with you for ever. KJV

11 2 Corinthians 1:3b-4a – The God of all comfort, who comforts us in all our troubles.

12 1 Peter 4:14b – The Spirit of glory and of God rests on you.

13 Romans 8:21 – Creation itself will be liberated from its bondage to decay and brought into the freedom and glory of the children of God.

20

Never Touch the Glory

What do you do when someone compliments you? Many of us are uncomfortable with receiving compliments. Responding can often be tricky, especially if you're a follower of Jesus. Do you accept the compliment ("Thank you; I appreciate your kind words."), downplay it ("I could have done better. I messed up a few times."), deflect it ("It's all God."), or try to escape it by changing the topic?

When we receive a compliment, we are on testing ground. Many times we work hard to attain some goal and it feels good to have other people recognize our efforts and approve of our achievement. Yet we realize we are called to be humble. Our response is a fine balance.

As Christians, we know God created us and in doing so, He gave each of us undeniable talents and abilities. We have certain economic, social, and societal advantages and varied proclivities. How all of this comes together is largely up to us. We are empty vessels that God can fill with His power to accomplish great things for eternal purposes.

> We are like clay jars in which
> this treasure is stored.
> The real power comes
> from God and not from us.
> 2 Corinthians 4:7, CEV

Andrew Murray, a South African pastor who lived over 100 years ago, stated, "The highest glory of the creature is in being a vessel, to receive and enjoy and show forth the glory of God. It can do this only as it is willing to be nothing in itself, that God may be everything. Water always fills first the lowest places. The lower, the emptier a man lies before God, the speedier and the fuller will be the inflow of the divine glory."[A] When we submit to God and allow Him to work through us with divine power, great things can happen. It can be very exciting. And likely others will notice and express their praise and appreciation. Nothing is wrong with that. It's what we do with the admiration that's important.

It's essentially a heart issue. A sincere expression of appreciation for a compliment is far better than false humility. But we will be wise to remember that pride is always waiting to raise its ugly head; and it will be our downfall. It displeases God when we take credit for what He does in us, as if our own skill, wisdom, and brilliance achieved such great success.

> "Never touch the glory;
> it belongs to God alone."
> A. Wetherell Johnson
> Missionary and founder of Bible Study Fellowship

God wants to use us and our life to achieve wonderful things for the Kingdom; and what a blessing to be able to watch His powerful hand at work in us. When someone sees something good in us, it's okay to accept the compliment, but we should be moved to thank God in prayer for what He did in our life. Anything worthy of praise ultimately comes from Him. Either verbally—if sincere—or privately we should glorify God and give Him all the credit. (We have all been around people who pompously deflect to God, but it often comes off as insincere and a ploy to gain even more admiration for themselves.)

> "To God alone belongs the glory—
> all of the credit, all of the attention,
> all of the applause."[B]
> Chuck Swindoll

The apostle Paul humbled himself to the Corinthian church, basically acknowledging he had no eloquence, wisdom, or abilities of his own. He admitted he was scared to death to preach. And his message and style of preaching were mediocre. He said it was because the Holy Spirit within him worked with such power that their faith rested on God.[1]

> We don't have the right to claim
> that we have done anything on our own.
> God gives us what it takes to do all that we do.
> 2 Corinthians 3:5, CEV

When believers are truly humble in heart and deflect the glory, it doesn't stop there. Pastor Warren W. Wiersbe once said, "There is no limit to what God will do for the believer who will let God have all the glory."[C]

The more we have been found faithful, the more God will entrust us with in the future. The more we honor God with the glory, not taking it for ourselves, the more He will bless and honor us in return.

Living for His *Glory*

But for you who honor Me,
goodness will shine on you like the sun.
Malachi 4:2a, NCV

That's the nature of humility. When we seek the position of humility on our knees in gratitude, the Lord lifts us up in honor.

Humble yourselves before the Lord
and he will exalt you.
James 4:10, CSB

Very few people have modeled this as well as lifelong evangelist, Billy Graham. He glorified God well and in turn, God brought honor back to him.

"All that I have been able to do,
I owe to Jesus Christ.
Any honors I have received,
I accept with a sense of inadequacy and humility,
and will reserve the right to hand
all of these someday to Christ,
when I see Him face-to-face."[D]
Billy Graham

---

[1] 1 Corinthians 2:1-5

114

21

~❧~

It is Well with My Soul

⚬

"When sorrows come,
they come not single spies,
but in battalions."
Claudius in Hamlet by William Shakespeare (1564-1616)

⚬

oratio Gates Spafford, Jr. (1828-1888) was born to
an extraordinary father, Horatio Sr. who was an
author, inventor, and editor. He corresponded
regularly with American leaders such as Thomas Jefferson,
John Adams, and James Madison. He was a man of
prominence and influence in the federal government.[A]

Horatio Jr. grew up to be a successful and affluent
attorney in a thriving law firm in Chicago in the mid-1800s.
He used most of his wealth serving God. He was an active
abolitionist and hosted numerous anti-slavery meetings in
his home. He served in prisons and ran numerous revivals.[B]
He was also trustee and benefactor of the Presbyterian
Theological Seminary of the Northwest.[C]

As an elder in a Presbyterian church,[D] Horatio was a
devoted Christian who loved God's Word. He taught a
Sunday School class for young people.[A] In his class one year
was Anna Larssen (1842-1923), a beautiful and intelligent
young Norwegian girl. He was shocked to learn that she was

only 15 years old, fourteen years younger than he was. He arranged and paid for her to attend a finishing school near Chicago for three years; upon graduation, they married. He was 33; she was 19. They moved into their new home, located on 12 acres north of Chicago; it was valued at $38,000 in 1870[A] (today's equivalent would be $775,000).

Horatio and Anna were devout Christians, very active in their church; they supported numerous Christian causes. They had many close friends who were evangelists including the famous Dwight L. Moody[A] who founded Moody Bible Institute and Moody Publishers.

The Spaffords were blessed with five children, four girls and a son. At four years of age, their son, Horatio, died suddenly of Scarlet Fever.[E]

Only a year later, the Great Chicago Fire swept through downtown Chicago in October 1871, burning wildly for two days until a drenching rain gave a needed boost to firefighting efforts.[F] It left more than 300 people dead with greater than 100,000 others homeless as over one third of the city crumbled to ash—utter devastation.[B] More than 17,000 structures were destroyed; damages were estimated at $200 million[F] (which equates to $4.2 billion today). The fire destroyed much of the downtown, in excess of four square miles. It was considered "one of the largest U.S. disasters of the 19th century."[A]

The Spaffords had a sizable investment in real estate along Lake Michigan's shoreline (known as "the Loop" today); they lost everything overnight in the fire, except for their home.[A] Despite their substantial financial loss, Horatio and Anna devoted two years to feeding and caring for the thousands of homeless people in dire need, using what remaining resources they had. They also contributed to the reconstruction efforts.[B]

Horatio Spafford   Anna Spafford

In 1873, Anna's health was failing due to stress. In November, Horatio decided his family needed a vacation to put the tragic loss of their son and the devastation of the fire behind them. They chose to travel by ship to Europe to visit friends and assist D.L. Moody with a revival in England. At the last minute, Horatio was detained with unexpected business, so he sent his wife and daughters on ahead, intending to follow a few days later. His family boarded the luxury ocean liner, the S. S. Ville Du Havre with high hopes of a much-needed respite with friends.[D]

The ship set sail to Paris on November 15, 1873. They endured six days of rough seas and finally awoke to a tranquil sea and beautiful weather. The evening was calm and spirits were high.[G]

On November 22, at about 2am, their ship collided with the Loch Earn, an iron sailing vessel,[C] just off the coast of Ireland[H] where the waters were three miles deep.[D] Passengers were jolted awake by what "sounded like two terrific claps of thunder."[G] Sparks shot out of the engine room like fireworks, tearing an enormous hole, 40 feet long and 10-20 feet deep, through the belly of the ship.[G]

Men, women, and children rushed about frantically, wearing only their nightshirts. Total pandemonium ensued as frigid water violently gushed forth, battering the sides of the steamer.[I] According to the Christian History Institute, "Anna Spafford and her daughters were seen huddled in one loving cluster."[A] Little Maggie, 9, was heard assuring her mother, "Mama, God will take care of us." Annie, the oldest at 11, sought to console her mother: "Don't be afraid. The sea is His and He made it."[G] Anna later wrote, "The dear children were so brave. They died praying."[J]

In one terrifying instant, the turbulent indigo ocean waters lacerated the struggling vessel, pitching everyone into its icy, foreboding waves. The pounding sea was brutal in its intensity as the ship thrashed about, shattering into scrap debris. Finally, the briny turbulence had its way and the ocean floor ultimately laid claim to the timbers and wreckage.

bb

The sinking of the iron steamship Ville du Havre

The ship sank in the Atlantic Ocean in only 12 minutes. Tragically, 226 of the 307 passengers and crew members lost their lives in this dreadful shipwreck, including the Spaffords' four daughters: Annie (age 11), Maggie (age 9), Bessie (age 5), and Tanetta (age 2). Their bodies were never found.[A]

Annie   Maggie   Bessie   Tanetta

cc

The Spafford daughters

Anna Spafford later wrote that she found peace with the situation. "How thankful I am that their little lives were so early dedicated to their Master."[K]

According to an account from the archives of the Christian History Institute,

> Anna Spafford later spoke of being sucked violently downward. Baby Tanetta was torn from her arms by a collision with some heavy debris, with a blow so violent that Anna's arm was severely bruised. She flailed at the water trying to catch her baby. Anna caught Tanetta's gown for just a moment before another smashing blow tore the little girl out of her arms forever...A young male passenger, afloat on a piece of wood, came upon Maggie and Annie, the two oldest Spafford children. At his direction, each girl grasped one of his side pockets as he tried to find a board large enough to support all three of

them. After about 30 or 40 minutes in the water, he found a piece of wreckage and struggled to help the two young girls climb atop the board. But as he watched, their weary arms weakened, and he saw their eyes close. Their lifeless forms floated away from his own fatigue-paralyzed arms. No clues ever surfaced about the fate of little Bessie.[A]

Anna was picked up unconscious, floating on a piece of wreckage.[E] The survivors were taken to Cardiff, Wales.[D] When able, Anna sent a telegram to her husband on December 1st that began with these heartbreaking words, "Saved alone. What shall I do…"[B] (Anna was only 31 at the time.)

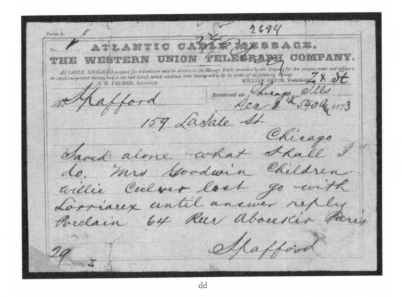

dd

Anna's telegram to Horatio

Some claim the sinking of the Ville du Havre was "the most tragic maritime disaster until the sinking of the *Titanic* in 1912."[C] Spafford boarded a ship to Wales to be with his wife. He told the captain that when they came to the place where the Ville du Havre went down, he wanted to be notified. On a dark, wintry cold December night, early in the morning, the captain knocked on Spafford's door to let him know they were passing by the place where the ship sank.[H]

Spafford walked out to the deck and stood in the freezing wind, the black inkiness of the sky engulfing him. He peered down at the swelling waters below—the watery grave of his precious daughters. He wept in despair over his lost children as he agonized over their tragic demise.

When he returned to his cabin, he could not sleep. Heartbroken, his soul swimming in grief, his mind overflowed with lyrics to what would become a great hymn to comfort many in the years to come. He quickly grabbed a pencil and scribbled the words as the Lord provided.

"When peace like a river attendeth my way, when sorrows like sea billows roll." He had just been gazing over the rails of the ship engrossed by the ocean's surging waves…the huge and undulant sea billows washing over the hull of the ship—a perfect metaphor for the agonizing sorrow flooding his soul.[H]

Philip Bliss (1838-1876), a gospel songwriter, composed the music for the lyrics in 1876.[A] This beloved hymn (initially entitled "Ville du Havre"—the name of the ship)[E] was sung for the first time in public (by Philip Bliss himself) on November 24, 1876 in Chicago for a large gathering of ministers, hosted by D.L. Moody. This was three years after the tragic shipwreck and ironically only one month before a devastating train wreck claimed the lives of Bliss and his wife.[A]

First print, 1876

In 1876, another son, also named Horatio, was born to them followed by Bertha two years later. In 1880, tragedy struck again. Little Horatio died at age four from Scarlet Fever, just like his brother of the same name years earlier. Their last child, Grace, was born shortly thereafter. [A,D]

With a deep interest in the Holy Land, the Spaffords moved to the old part of Jerusalem.[D] They found a large house in the Muslim Quarter, near Herod's Gate. Located on a hill, they could see the areas where they ministered: the Mohammedan, Muslim, and Jewish slums.[L] They cared for orphans, the homeless, the sick, and the needy.[H] Later, this Christian society they established became known as the "American Colony." They ran soup kitchens, orphanages, and hospitals.[L]

Horatio Spafford died in his sleep of Malaria on October 16, 1888 at age 59, leaving behind Anna and their daughters, Bertha (10) and Grace (8). After his death, Anna continued to work in the areas surrounding Jerusalem until her health failed. She died at age 80 in 1923.[L] Both were buried in Jerusalem.[E]

————

"I am glad to be able to trust my Lord
when it costs me something."
Horatio Gates Spafford

Today

Spafford descendants continue the ministry within the Damascus Gate of the Old City.[H] The Spafford Children's Center is still in existence, arising out of the American Colony in Jerusalem. They provide medical care and outreach services to Arab children and their families.[L] They care for over 30,000 needy children every year.[A] (http://www.spaffordcenter.org). The Spaffords' home is now The American Colony Hotel which continually ranks among the finest hotels in the world.[M]

God transformed the Spaffords' suffering into a ministry that helped tens of thousands of people in need[A] and brought countless souls to salvation through faith in Jesus.[L] God redeemed suffering for joy, ashes for beauty.

Although the hymn, "It is Well with My Soul," begins with loss, it embraces peace, and ends in radiant hope for that glorious day when our "faith shall be sight" at the Lord's triumphant return!

————

You will keep in perfect peace those whose minds
are steadfast, because they trust in you.
Isaiah 26:3

It Is Well with My Soul

Stanza 1

When peace like a river attendeth my way,
When sorrows like sea billows roll;
Whatever my lot, Thou hast taught me to say,
It is well, it is well with my soul.

—⁂—

Chorus:

It is well (it is well)
With my soul (with my soul).
It is well, it is well with my soul.

—⁂—

Stanza 2

Though Satan should buffet,
though trials should come,
Let this blest assurance control,
That Christ has regarded my helpless estate,
And has shed His own blood for my soul.

Stanza 3

My sin, oh the bliss of this glorious thought!
My sin, not in part, but the whole,
Is nailed to the cross, and I bear it no more,
Praise the Lord, praise the Lord, O my soul!

Stanza 4

And Lord, haste the day
when my faith shall be sight,
The clouds be rolled back as a scroll;
The trump shall resound, and the Lord shall descend,
Even so, it is well with my soul!

22

~o~

Do You Want to Get Well?

$\mathcal{I}$t all happened during one of the annual Jewish festivals in Jerusalem. Near the Sheep Gate there was a pool. Here many people would lie, day after day—people with disabilities: blind, lame, paralyzed. This wasn't just any ordinary pool; it was seen as a special pool by the people who lived there. Pastor John MacArthur notes, "Some ancient witnesses indicate that the waters of the pool were red with minerals, and thus thought to have medicinal value."[A]. It was believed that an angel stirred the waters every day, imparting healing powers. The people believed that after the water was stirred, the first person in the water would be healed.[B]

There was a certain man who had been lying there 38 years. The Bible describes him as an invalid. We don't know any other details; we don't even know his name. He likely was paralyzed in some way or perhaps had a disability that affected his ability to walk. From the outside looking in, his situation was hopeless. The man was miserable.

One day, Jesus ventured by and saw the man lying there. He stopped and learned of his condition. Then Jesus did a peculiar thing. He asked the man, "Do you want to get well?"[1] The man exuded tremendous frustration and defeat. He answered by explaining that he has no one to help him and others rush ahead of him to the pool as the water bubbles and gurgles up. He was exhausted from trying so hard day after day.

Jesus didn't join him in his misery. Instead, He made a startling charge: "Get up! Pick up your mat and walk."[2] It was audacious!

The man was taken aback. He had a choice to make:

1. Continue to wallow in his pit of self-pity.
2. Trust this man who offered hope and obey his command.

Thankfully, we see that he chose the 2nd option. And he was cured. He picked up his mat and walked away! (Read the story in John 5:1-15.) Notice that Jesus didn't physically take him to the pool at Bethesda; that's because the Living Water came to him!

How are you Paralyzed?

Are you paralyzed in an area of your life? Are you tired of trying so hard to bring about change? In many ways, we are as lifeless as this man was. Enter in Living Hope. When Jesus walks in, we have a choice to make. Either we stay where we are in the pit of self-pity, or we turn to God in submission, trust, and obedience. When the Living Water comes to us, we get the opportunity to accept the new life He offers as grace rushes in unabated.

Apart from God, we are as helpless spiritually as this man was physically. Jesus could have healed this man with just a word. But instead, Jesus challenged him to act. He wanted him to participate in bringing about the miracle! He was not told to try harder, but to trust. He was told to pick up his mat.

Likewise, God does not tell us to try harder. In fact, He asks us to quit trying so hard and to trust. Sometimes our trying gets in the way of our trusting. "Trust Me," he says with compassion as He extends His hand toward us. Pick up your mat (carry your responsibilities) and step out in faith toward a new life. As lifeless as this man was, so are we until we accept new life from God.

Would I help?

A lady I know needed help with a relationship in her life. Over coffee one day, I met with her; she opened up to me about her struggles. I listened intently, then asked her one simple question, "Do you want to get well?" She looked surprised and said she did. I gave her the counseling number for an international ministry as well as phone numbers for local counselors. She said she would call.

A month later, she seemed to be just as discouraged as before. When asked, she admitted that she had not gotten around to calling any of the phone numbers I provided. Nor had she done so several months later. Today, she seems just as frustrated and hopeless, if not more so, than she was when we first met.

She did not want to get well.

Do the hard thing

I have a family member who struggles with an addiction. Like with my friend, I asked him one day, "Do you want to get well?" He replied, "Yes. Who would answer 'no' to that?" Great question. I told him that most people answer "No." When a person decides he wants to get well, it comes at a cost, and it can be terrifying. There's nothing easy about it. He must be willing to face the problem head-on, confront the issue, pick up his mat of responsibility in the situation, and do what it takes to get well.

- Admit you need help.
- Make that phone call.
- Go to counseling.
- Go to rehab.
- Pour out the alcohol.
- Go to the doctor.
- Spend the money.
- Put away the gaming system.
- Agree to the surgery.
- Apply for the job.
- Get off the internet.
- Invest your time.
- Ask for forgiveness.
- Seek restoration in that relationship.

Getting well requires courage. It's often easier to continue as you've been doing because it's comfortable, rather than commit to what it takes to get well. Getting well requires effort and usually involves pain and discomfort; it can be very hard.

It takes guts to admit you have a problem with your child and call that counselor. It takes grit to come to terms with your pornography or drug addiction and reach out for hope. Rehab is long and hard. It takes strength to divulge your weakness to yourself and others. It takes courage to disclose that your marriage is in trouble. Surgery hurts. Chemo has side effects. It takes mettle to bare your soul to another. Spontaneous miracles still occur today: the taste for alcohol suddenly goes away, the tumor mysteriously disappears, the lawsuit is dropped. But I don't want to pretend to offer false hope. Usually "getting well" is a process—and a painful one at that.

I would be remiss if I failed to mention that believers will always get well, but sometimes our healing occurs on the other side of heaven.

Spiritual effects of sin

A short while later, Jesus ran into this same man at the temple and said to him, "You are well again. Stop sinning or something worse may happen to you."[3] The man was physically healed, but still had a spiritual affliction; he needed to stop sinning. We all have the same spiritual condition. With humility and the strength of the Holy Spirit, we must resolve to do what it takes to stop the sin in our lives. We must choose to get well.

---

[1] John 5:6b
[2] John 5:8b
[3] John 5:14b

23

~

Getting Well

When we decide we want to get well, we start with prayer. As we approach God Almighty and His holiness in repentance, our posture must be one of humble reverence. God will show us the sin in our lives and will lead us to wholeness—to getting well.

In his book, *Too Busy Not to Pray*, Pastor Bill Hybels tells a story about a motorcycle.

> A motorcycle is a rugged machine that can take incredible abuse, but its fuel has to be pure. At refueling time I would pour the fuel through a filter or a handkerchief to be sure no contaminants would prevent the engine from running at its full potential. Any speck of dirt could cause a loss of power.[A]

He goes on to say that our Christian life is similar to the motorcycle. If we let even a speck of sin into our heart, it will contaminate our prayers. "God," he says, "expects us to maintain strict personal integrity."[C] If we refuse to walk with God in humility and with integrity and instead choose to live with active, willful sin in our lives, "We are presumptuous to expect God to answer our prayers. If you're tolerating sin in your life, don't waste your breath praying unless it's a prayer of confession. Receive the

Lord's forgiveness and then he will listen when you pour out your heart to him"[A]

God doesn't hear our prayers when we persist in sinning, knowing it's wrong. When we continue to live in sin, we place a wall between us and God. We obviously can't remember every sin we commit, but our attitude should be one of humility and confession. Sin offends our holy God and cuts us off from Him. He cannot ignore or tolerate sin but expects us to repent so He can forgive and cleanse us from all unrighteousness. If, however, we choose to continue to live in sin, He won't answer our prayers.

Are you living with your boyfriend? Are you getting drunk every weekend? Are you viewing pornography? Are you acting selfishly? Are you lying about what you're doing in your free time? Are you cheating in school or on your taxes? Are you being unfaithful to your spouse? What can be found in your internet search history? Are you hooking up? Is your language disrespectful of His holiness? Is your anger out of control? Do you treat the underprivileged as "less than?" If so, God will not hear your pleas. Repent with a broken heart, then reach out to Him and He will listen.

> If I had cherished sin in my heart,
> The Lord would not have listened.
> Psalm 66:18

> But your sins have separated you from your God.
> They have caused him to turn his face away from you.
> So he won't listen to you.
> Isaiah 59:2, NIRV

When Jesus was nailed to the cross, all of our sins—past, present, and future—were placed on Him and He *became* the complete sacrifice for our sins. He was banished from the presence of God because sin cannot exist in God's presence.[1] Separation from God is exceedingly painful. Sin *always* leads to separation, sometimes from other people, but always from God. Praise God that Jesus endured the separation from God that you and I deserve.

Receive the Lord's forgiveness, then He will listen when you pour out your heart to Him.

Your guidelines for living—are they from God or yourself? If they are from yourself, they won't work. You'll find yourself back at that pool, sitting on the sidelines of life—helpless, defeated, and without hope. Health and wholeness require courageous responsibility to bring your life in alignment with God's will.

Some important points to note:

- Jesus went to where the broken people were, instead of where the important, powerful people gathered. He still does that today. Jesus isn't impressed by power, status, job title, accolades, awards, bank accounts, race, spheres of influence, or the car you drive. He cares about the condition of your heart and soul—your brokenness.

- Being paralyzed in fear or hopelessness is truly incapacitating. It is all-consuming and exhausting! At this stage, there is NO JOY left. You need help. Invite Jesus to enter in. He will listen to every word you utter and won't get distracted. He sees your tears but won't force Himself on you. If you are drowning in a pit of self-pity, he won't rebuke you, but will pour out compassion for your suffering. Cry when you need to. Take time to process the grief and the hurt.

Then it's time

But then you must move on. Quit looking down; look up! Do you see Jesus standing with tears in His eyes, waiting for you to reach out to Him? Smiling, He asks, "Do you want to get well?" Answer carefully. If you decide it's time to get well, realize it comes with a price. The healing of the invalid was conditional upon him doing what Jesus directed: step out in faith and obedience. Radical life change requires radical choices.

The time has come to trust Jesus. You don't have to suffer alone. Take Jesus by the hand as "He leads [you] beside still waters."[2] Feel Him lift you out of the pit of self-pity and helplessness where the raging currents of surging emotions threaten to pull you under—time and time again. Pick up your mat, carry your responsibilities, and move forward in faith as God leads…

Then bask in cool refreshment as splashes of Living Water envelop you. Living Water—the only thing with the power to heal you. Can you hear the splatter of wet goodness drenching your being? Can you feel the splashes of healing as your soul is revitalized and joy starts to rejuvenate your spirit? Bask in the soothing bounty and allow the Living Water of Christ to saturate your soul down to its very essence—right where healing begins.

It's time to get well, don't you think?

---

[1] Mark 15:34b – Jesus cried out in a loud voice, "Eloi, Eloi, lama sabachthani?"–which means, "My God, my God, why have you forsaken me?"

[2] Psalm 23:2b, ESV

24

Be There—Nothing Else Matters

It was supposed to be fun.

It was supposed to start with a warm handshake
and end with a cool drink.

It was only a game.

It wasn't supposed to end this way.

But it did.

*P*istol Pete. A basketball legend. The NCAA's all-time
leading scorer (by a large margin) in three years at
Louisiana State University[A] where he averaged an
astounding 44.2 points per game. Then a ten-year career in
the NBA where he averaged 24.2 points per game with the
Atlanta Hawks, New Orleans Jazz, and Boston Celtics.[B]
Did I mention that he was a five-time NBA All Star?[A] Or
that he was inducted into the Hall of Fame in 1987?
Legendary Coach John Wooden called him "the greatest
ballhandler he ever saw." And in 1997, "Maravich was
selected as one of the 50 greatest players in NBA history."[B]
But perhaps he was best known as the ultimate showman
with his crazy moves and special flair.[A] He made the game
fun and highly entertaining for his many fans. He often shot
the ball from his side, as if holding a revolver. Thus the
nickname "Pistol Pete" was born!

His real name: Peter Maravich. Five years before he died, he became a born-again Christian and traveled the country sharing his story. In January 1988, James Dobson, president of Focus on the Family ministry, invited Maravich to do a segment with him on his syndicated radio show.[B]

Dobson had been playing rec basketball three days/week with a group of guys and got the outlandish idea that perhaps Maravich might like to play with them. Pistol Pete readily agreed.[B] On Tuesday, January 5th, 1988, on a chilly winter day in Colorado Springs, nine guys took to the court. After about 45 minutes of a light-hearted half-court game at the First Church of the Nazarene, they took a break. Maravich walked up to Dobson. Knowing he hadn't played in a year, Dobson asked Maravich how he was feeling. He replied, "I feel great, I feel fine." Then he took one step and collapsed. Despite CPR, they couldn't revive Pistol Pete. The legendary showman died on the floor.[A] He was only 40 years old. It turns out, "He had been born without one of the two artery systems that supply the heart with blood." This led to "deterioration of the tissues in his heart."[B]

"How ironic," Dobson noted, "that he was wearing a T-shirt that said, 'Looking unto Jesus,' because he was at that moment looking unto Jesus. He saw Him face to face."[C]

Later that day, Dobson sat down with his 17-year-old son, Ryan. With the magnitude of what had occurred earlier that day weighing heavily on his mind, Dobson was somber as he relayed the tragic event to his son. "I told him that what happened to Pete wasn't an isolated event. This is the human condition. This is all of us. It will happen to me some day."[D] With an intense urgency, he continued, "Pete Maravich didn't have an opportunity to speak with his family one last time. But I want to tell you, be there. On resurrection morning, be there. I will be looking for you then. Nothing else matters. Be there."[D]

Just two years later, Dobson collapsed on the same basketball court with a heart attack.[D] Thankfully, he recovered. He still speaks and gives graduation addresses from time to time and relays this experience to his captivated audiences. "Be there. Nothing else matters."

Do you know without a doubt, that when you die, you will go to heaven? If not, make peace with God right now. This is the most important decision you will ever make. Decide this day whom you will serve. Will you serve God or will you serve yourself?

25

~∾~

Whose Glory?

*I*t was his senior year at the University of Florida. Tim Tebow was greatly anticipating the upcoming, highly televised Bowl Championship Series between Florida and Oklahoma. It was 2009. And Tebow, 21 years old, felt God was leading him to do something a bit radical during this game. As senior quarterback for the Florida Gators, he wore *John 3:16* etched in eye-black for the world to see while he played his heart out for the championship. Why John 3:16? "It's the essence of our hope," he replied.[A] This is the verse he boldly broadcasted during that game, without ever saying a word:

> For God so loved the world
> that he gave his one and only Son,
> that whoever believes in him
> shall not perish
> but have eternal life.
> John 3:16

After winning the championship, Tebow was told that during the game, 94 million people googled John 3:16. That's remarkable in itself, but that's not all.[A]

Fast forward exactly three years

To the very day. It was January 9, 2012. Tebow was now a Denver Broncos quarterback. The underdog Broncos had just defeated the mighty Pittsburgh Steelers in the NFL playoffs. As Tim Tebow was heading into the post-game press conference, his public relations representative met him with wide-eyed astonishment. It wasn't just a playoff win in overtime. It was far bigger…far more significant! He proceeded to enlighten Tebow about what *really* happened.

"During the game," he excitedly disclosed, "you threw for 316 yards, your yards per completion were 31.6 [highest in NFL postseason history], your yards per rush were 3.16, the [CBS's final] ratings for the night were 31.6, and the time of possession was 31:06, and during the game 91 million people googled John 3:16 and it's the number one trending thing on every platform."[A] A radio show commentator brought these numbers to light on his program one afternoon and was later informed that he began the discussion at 3:16pm that day.[B]

Just a mere coincidence? I think not.

The odds of Tebow pulling these exact numbers is over 5.24 billion to one.[B] Divine intervention? I believe so.

And…there's a little bit more! His coach's name was John and Tebow threw the winning pass to Demaryius Thomas, a guy born on Christmas day in 1987.

Tebow froze in shocked silence. "I was just standing there in the hallway about to do this press conference just thinking that that night was about a football game. It really wasn't…we serve such a big God." Tebow believes God displayed a miracle that night. "The God that we serve is a God of miracles," he continued. "I just have to be willing to step out and say, 'Here you go, God, I'm going to give you my fish and my loaves of bread and watch what [You do] with it.'"A

Tim Tebow has chosen to live his life, not aimlessly, but with purpose. And that purpose is to give glory to God in all he does. Not just in some things. But in ALL things.

- Does it matter to him if people find him odd? *Not at all.*
- Does it matter if people criticize him or bring accusations against him? *Not a bit.*
- Does he care what others think? *Not in the least.*

The only thing that matters is the God he serves—that God's glory be exalted.

For nearly two years, Tim Tebow etched many Bible verses on his eye-black. These became a type of personal spiritual billboard, if you will. In addition to John 3:16, already cited, he also etched the following verses on his eye-black.D, E, F

Keep this Book of the Law always on your lips;
meditate on it day and night,
so that you may be careful
to do everything written in it.
Then you will be prosperous and successful.
Have I not commanded you?
Be strong and courageous.
Do not be terrified;
do not be discouraged,
for the LORD your God will be
with you wherever you go.
Joshua 1:8-9

Living for His *Glory*

The LORD is my shepherd,
I lack nothing.
Psalm 23:1

———

Trust in the LORD with all your heart
and lean not on your own understanding;
in all your ways submit to him,
and he will make your paths straight.
Proverbs 3:5-6

———

Those who hope in the LORD
will renew their strength.
They will soar on wings like eagles;
they will run and not grow weary,
they will walk and not be faint.
Isaiah 40:31

———

What good is it for someone to gain
the whole world, yet forfeit their soul?
Mark 8:36

———

I have told you these things,
so that in me you may have peace.
In this world you will have trouble.
But take heart! I have overcome the world.
John 16:33

———

I am not ashamed of the gospel,
because it is the power of God that brings
salvation to everyone who believes.
Romans 1:16a

And we know that in all things
God works for the good of those
who love him, who have
been called according to his purpose.
Romans 8:28

Be kind and compassionate to one another,
forgiving each other,
just as in Christ God forgave you.
Ephesians 4:32

Do not be anxious about anything,
but in every situation, by prayer and petition,
with thanksgiving,
present your requests to God.
And the peace of God,
which transcends all understanding,
will guard your hearts
and your minds in Christ Jesus.
Philippians 4:6-7

I can do all things through
Christ who strengthens me.
Philippians 4:13, NKJV

Whatever you do, work heartily,
as to the Lord, and not to men.
Colossians 3:23, ESV

Give thanks in all circumstances,
for this is God's will for you in Christ Jesus.
1 Thessalonians 5:18

Therefore, since we are surrounded by
so great a cloud of witnesses,
let us lay aside every weight,
and the sin which so easily ensnares us,
and let us run with endurance
the race that is set before us,
looking unto Jesus,
the author and finisher of our faith,
who for the joy that was set before Him
endured the cross,
despising the shame
and has sat down at the right hand
of the throne of God.
Hebrews 12:1-2, NKJV

Consider it pure joy,
my brothers and sisters,
whenever you face trials of many kinds,
because you know that
the testing of your faith
produces perseverance.
Let perseverance finish its work
so that you may be mature and complete,
not lacking anything.
James 1:2-4

Interestingly, the practice of putting on eye-black beneath the eyes with words, numbers, logos, or symbols was banned by the NCAA in April 2010. It was immediately dubbed the "Tim Tebow Rule." (The NCAA denies that Tebow's messages triggered the change.)[c]

His last message etched in eye-black was:

> For it is by grace you have been saved,
> through faith—and this not from yourselves,
> it is the gift of God—
> not by works, so that no one can boast.
> For we are God's handiwork,
> created in Christ Jesus to do good works,
> which God prepared in advance for us to do.
> Ephesians 2:8-10

Let's get personal

You may not use eye-black beneath your eyes for all to see. But you wear the imprint of whom or what you serve every single day. People are watching you, perhaps not 91 million but significantly more than you realize, to see what makes you tick—to determine your purpose. What does the world see when they watch you? What values does your life portray?

Don't discount the influence you have. We all influence someone and likely many more than that! Make sure that when you're playing your life's game, the watching world sees something worth checking out.

Are you living for God's Glory or your own? Only God's glory lasts for eternity. Our personal "little g" glory dies when we do. Choose carefully.

If you chose to broadcast a Bible verse to the watching world, which verse would you choose?

26

Unshakable Peace

For many years, my mom and I shared an expression when things went wrong. "There's no peace!" we'd exclaim dramatically. One day, I found a little polished stone on which *peace* was imprinted. I gave it to her at lunch one day. "Now you have peace," I cheerfully proclaimed. She promptly lost the stone.

Peace can be so elusive. It is something everyone yearns for, yet few ever find. In our world where the use of antidepressant drugs has increased at an astounding rate, we realize many people are depressed, anxious, and fearful, desperate for a deep, abiding inner peace for their troubled souls.

The Bible isn't silent on this topic. The word, *peace*, is found 420 times in the King James Bible.

Life is fraught with plenty of trouble.[1] No one comes out unscathed. As we struggle to cope, peace seems far away. Challenges flood in the front door and peace takes off running through the back door. Peace escapes from three different sources:

- Our past—our regrets
- Our present—our current problems and stress
- Our future—our fears and anxieties about the many "what ifs" that loom ahead of us

How we cope

We all have our vices, things we resort to as we try to deal with (or avoid) our stress. We mistakenly think these vices will bring us peace.

- Some people drink until they're so numb, they can no longer feel the pain in their hearts. Others use drugs for the same effect.
  It doesn't last. And they only feel awful when the effects wane.
- Some hop from one relationship to the next—to the next—to the next, hoping someone will fill the void.
  No one ever does. They only get additional baggage heaped on top of their current baggage.
- For others, peace means staying busy all the time, so they collapse into bed at night with no energy left to think.
  This is futile and exhausting.
- Some shop excessively to distract themselves from the stress in their lives.
  This only causes more stress as bills mount and there are more things to take care of.
- Many people overeat or gorge on chocolate or ice cream to drown their cares.
  This only leads to added pounds, feelings of defeat, and increased health issues.
- Others immerse themselves in New Age gimmicks, such as healing crystals, tarot card readings, or aromatherapy.
  They soon find this is all a dead end.
- Countless people binge watch television shows or get hooked on video games for hours on end.
  This, too, is empty and leaves behind feelings of hopelessness and isolation.

The world offers deceptive, false peace which is short-lived and unreliable. All of our earthly vices are hollow and temporary; they don't change our circumstances nor drive away our problems. They are based on tactics of escape and diversions. They may help for the moment but will come up woefully short by adding additional stress and problems. And they delay the inevitable. Problems still need to be dealt with.

If we place our security in the things of this world, whenever our situation changes, our peace vanishes and is replaced with anxiety, frustration, and fear.

Real peace

Most people don't have the foggiest idea what peace really is. God's peace is superior to anything the world can offer. In *My Utmost for His Highest*, Oswald Chambers tells us that "Peace is not the absence of trouble. Peace is the presence of God."[A] Within the pages of our Bibles, we find that real peace is:

- Knowing that no matter what we do, Jesus will never stop loving us.
- Knowing that no matter where we go, He goes too.
- Remembering He will never leave us…no matter what.
- Knowing that no matter what happens, God will give us the strength and grace to cope.
- Living by God's Word—our guidebook—which avoids a lot of the hurts and habits that mess up lives.
- Trusting Christ to forgive us of all past mistakes and not remember them anymore. They are gone! Past regrets are no more.
- Accepting God's wisdom to handle our current problems as He walks with us to the other side.

- Living in confidence that God promises to be in our future, guiding us and helping us, so we have no need to fear. Our future rests in eternity with Him because He has conquered death.

The world will bring us struggles, problems, and strife until Jesus returns. When we focus on our troubles, we allow fear and anxiety to dominate our minds (where they quickly multiply). Peace will be absent. Every. Single. Time.

Yet God promises us peace when we keep our eyes on Jesus and trust His promises; in Him is our security. Despite how things look, He has our best interests at heart and is working everything out for our good and His glory.[2]

Submitting to the Lord replaces our inner turmoil with quiet trust and an internal calm despite our circumstances. If we place our security in God, who never changes, our peace is unshakable.

Jesus is all we need for true peace.

---

[1] John 16:33b – In this world, you will have trouble.

[2] Romans 8:28 – We know that in all things God works for the good of those who love him, who have been called according to his purpose.

27

So Many Lights

Lily, our white toy poodle, had developed renal failure. We were giving her subcutaneous fluids during the day so consequently, she had to go to the bathroom more frequently. Not wanting to get up in the middle of the night, we put down a pad in the laundry room for her use. She also has limited vision. In order to help her navigate the path to her pad in the wee hours of the night, we kept the hall light on as well as the light in the laundry room.

One day, as I was doing laundry, I looked up at the light. I was startled to see quite a number of bugs inside the fixture…all dead. As I pondered this, I was struck by how sad this was. The bugs were attracted to the light at night and drawn to it, only to find themselves marching to their death unaware. The very thing that enticed and captivated them was that which caused their demise.

It's like that today in our human world. There are so many lights that draw us in. They captivate us; something about them attracts us. Maybe it's the light of scientology, or the light of the New Age movement, or possibly the light of Islam. Perhaps the light of atheism…or Mormonism. There has recently been an astronomical rise in the number of people who are drawn to the light of the Wicca movement or pagan witchcraft.

So many lights; they all hold something that catches our attention. Sadly, some people are drawn to them—to their peril. The very thing that gets their attention and allures them actually leads them to their death—eternal death.

The true Light

Jesus became the Light of the world—the only true Light of salvation.

> I am the light of the world.
> Whoever follows me will never walk in darkness,
> but will have the light of life.
> John 8:12b

His light draws us to everlasting life. All other lights we pursue are fake (false prophets or teachers often tempting us to follow them to disastrous destinations) which lead to everlasting death. In His Sermon on the Mount, Jesus made a stunning declaration:

> You are the light of the world.
> Matthew 5:14a

That's rather shocking! We are created in His image, so Jesus is passing along His identity and corresponding responsibility to us! Only Christ is the true Light. We are like lanterns; Christ is the Light inside. We are holders of the Light. Can you begin to wrap your mind around the magnitude of this honor?

> You were once darkness, but now you are
> light in the Lord. Live as children of light.
> Ephesians 5:8

Let's never forget our identity. We don't belong to the darkness of this world; we belong to the light.

> You are all children of the light and children of the day.
> We do not belong to the night or to the darkness.
> So then, let us not be like others, who are asleep,
> but let us be awake and sober.
> Since we belong to the day, let us be sober,
> putting on faith and love as a breastplate,
> and the hope of salvation as a helmet.
> 1 Thessalonians 5:5-6, 8

Many false lights

The Bible contains many references of caution instructing us to be vigilant and watchful. We are warned to be careful of people leading us to false hope rooted in different religions and the occult. Know what you believe and why you believe it so you can effectively heed the many warnings in Scripture.

> Blessed is the one who trusts in the LORD,
> who does not look to the proud,
> to those who turn aside to false gods.
> Psalm 40:4

———

> Watch out for false prophets.
> They come to you in sheep's clothing,
> but inwardly they are ferocious wolves.
> Matthew 7:15

———

> False messiahs and false prophets
> will appear...to deceive.
> Mark 13:22

Such people are false apostles, deceitful workers,
masquerading as apostles of Christ.
And no wonder, for Satan himself
masquerades as an angel of light.
2 Corinthians 11:13-14

There were also false prophets among the people,
just as there will be false teachers among you.
2 Peter 2:1a

Dear friends, do not believe every spirit,
but test the spirits to see whether they are from God,
because many false prophets
have gone out into the world.
1 John 4:1

We all shine

Here's the bottom line: we all shine light. Whatever light we choose to follow is the light we reflect and shine into a lost and floundering world of darkness, desperately in need of the One pure and true Light of salvation. What light do you shine? Make sure you shine the Light of Christ—the Light of Truth. Light brings hope and clarity to the confusion and despair of the darkness. You know that song, "This little light of mine, I'm gonna let it shine…"

That's exactly what we're called to do. It's in our DNA to SHINE!

Keep your flame bright and shine with the hope that is within you! Shine with boldness! Shine with JOY for His glory! What a blessed responsibility and privilege!

28

I am Worn Out Because…

*H*ave you ever pleaded with God to change your circumstances? What heavy burdens have you been carrying for a long time? I recently asked some friends to complete this sentence, "I am worn out because…" What great responses I received. Here's a sampling:

- I have poor boundaries.
- I'm worried about everything and everybody.
- No matter how hard I try, it is never enough.
- Days are long.
- I take on the emotions of others.
- Human suffering.
- Lack of love shown for one another.
- Chronic pain.
- Life is overwhelming and too hard.
- Chemotherapy/radiation.
- School.
- I try to be everything to everybody, even when I know it's impossible.
- I try to be perfect in an imperfect world.
- My marriage tries my soul.
- The world is a mess.

You're not alone. We all feel it. We all get weary. The Lord is well-acquainted with our design; He had everything to do with it. He knew from the very beginning that we would get worn out. We grow weary because we live in these frail bodies—on this broken earth—in these frustrating circumstances—with people who hurt us, annoy us, and disappoint us. And it all makes us tired—very tired.

So what do you do when you're weary—worn out? A movie? The driving range? A manicure? Netflix? Call someone? Alcohol? Shopping? Gardening?

Or perhaps you're trying to counter it ahead of time to avoid getting weary. Vitamins. Exercise. Cultivation of friendships. More sleep. Healthy food. Better organization. A personal retreat. All well and good, but these aren't the answer.

The Lord tells us, "In your worn out, know where to go." (my words)

> [The LORD] will not grow tired or weary,
> and his understanding no one can fathom.
> He gives strength to the weary
> and increases the power of the weak.
> Even youths grow tired and weary,
> and young men stumble and fall;
> but those who hope in the LORD
> will renew their strength.
> They will soar on wings like eagles;
> they will run and not grow weary,
> they will walk and not be faint.
> Isaiah 40:28b-31

God assures us that He is incapable of growing weary and doesn't need sleep.[1] What a relief that He is always on

His throne, orchestrating the workings of the universe, tending to His flock, answering our prayers—while never fatiguing. Yet He acknowledges that because we were created with limits, we will all get weary.

To the weary, He says, "Do you want renewed strength?" "Do you want Me to help you endure?" When we're depleted and we've got nothing left, Isaiah tells us to put our hope in the Lord. Hope is bold; it is solid confidence and trust of a sure expectation. Then He makes an unbelievable offer—a conditional promise we can count on. When we put our hope in the Lord, He renews our strength, but in a most unusual way. The Hebrew word for *renew* is "to exchange." It's like taking off our old coat of weakness and weary and exchanging it for His brand-new coat of strength and power. God alone can restore our soul.

We serve a big God who has it under control. His plan is to renew our strength so we can soar on wings like eagles and not grow weary. In the Bible, the eagle is regarded as the greatest of birds. We won't just "get by," we will soar! Warren Wiersbe sums it up well, "As we wait before Him, God enables us to soar when there is a crisis, to run when the challenges are many, and to walk faithfully in the day-by-day demands of life."[A]

It is a misrepresentation of this life to believe we will come to a place one day where we will not get worn out. There is a recurring weariness inherent in living on this earth as our bodies are finite. It is as unavoidable as breathing. We are inclined toward becoming worn out.

Perhaps you are taking on too many of life's battles yourselves. Are you overcommitted with a schedule jam-packed with no margin for rest? If so, your life is off-balance. Cease striving so hard. Re-center your life by seeking God. Make sure your steps align with His; don't run ahead of Him and His plan. Your hope rests in Him and Him alone. He is offering you a holy exchange which comes with a renewing of strength and new mercies so you will not only make it through the day, but soar. When you are at your weakest, God's power is at its strongest.[2] Let this be your confident hope.

When is the last time you asked the One whose power is unlimited to renew your dwindling strength?

[1] Psalm 121:4b – [The LORD]…will neither slumber nor sleep.
[2] 2 Corinthians 12:9b – My power is made perfect in weakness.

29

❧

Sin and Shame

*D*id you realize that when Jesus hung on the cross, He was unclothed?[1] I had always believed He sported a loin cloth or other such garment. But that's not true. Imagine His embarrassment as he hung on the cross, exposed in front of everyone, including His mother and the women at the cross.

Yet when I think about it, I understand. After Adam and Eve sinned in the Garden, they were filled with shame. They suddenly became aware of their nakedness and hid.

When we sin, we experience shame. We feel naked in our shame. Exposed. Sin and shame go hand in hand. And we stand condemned in our sin.

When Jesus was crucified, He not only took your sin and my sin upon His shoulders, but also the sin of the entire world—past, present, and future. And He took it a step further; He actually *became* our sin.[2] Not only did Jesus take all our sins, but our shame was heaped upon Him in abundance as well. He literally had the weight of the world upon Him as He valiantly went to the cross.

The judgment

When we face Christ at our death, we won't be wearing our spiffy outfits or our fine-looking khakis and pullover. We will stand before him as we are.

If we aren't believers, we will be naked before God in our shame. All we've ever done will be laid out, exposed, before our Savior.

If we are repentant believers, we will be wearing Jesus's robe of righteousness—not just any robe, but His very robe—which He gave us as a gift.[3]

We will never have to stand naked before God (or anyone else) when we have placed our faith in Jesus. The sin is forgiven[4] and forgotten.[5] The shame is gone. So is all condemnation.[6] We are free!

To God be all glory!

---

[1] Luke 23:34b – They divided up his clothes by casting lots.

[2] 2 Corinthians 5:21 - God made him who had no sin to be sin for us, so that in him we might become the righteousness of God.

[3] Isaiah 61:10b - For [the Lord] has clothed me with garments of salvation and arrayed me in a robe of his righteousness.

[4] Mathew 26:28 - This is my blood of the covenant, which is poured out for many for the forgiveness of sins.

[5] Hebrews 8:12 – I will forgive their wickedness and will remember their sins no more.

[6] Romans 8:1 – There is now no condemnation for those who are in Christ Jesus.

30

Caught Up in the Air

$\mathcal{I}$t had never happened before. It must have been frightening for his family left behind. He was there one moment; he was gone the next! Never to be seen again.

> Enoch walked faithfully with God;
> then he was no more,
> because God took him away.
> Genesis 5:24

> By faith Enoch was taken from this life,
> so that he did not experience death;
> he could not be found,
> because God had taken him away.
> For before he was taken,
> he was commended as one who pleased God.
> Hebrews 11:5

Enoch was the great-great-great-great-grandson of Adam. (Don't confuse this Enoch with Enoch, the son of Cain and grandson of Adam and Eve.) Enoch is one of two men in Scripture who never died. Both Enoch and Elijah were taken straight to heaven alive. Enoch appears in Genesis and we are told very little about him. It seems that as soon as he enters the scene, he is taken from the world and deposited into heaven. Enoch is an example of what will happen during the rapture.

We believe that Jesus died and rose again
and so we believe that God will bring with Jesus
those who have fallen asleep in him.

According to the Lord's word,
we tell you that we who are still alive,
who are left until the coming of the Lord,
will certainly not precede those
who have fallen asleep.

For the Lord himself will come down
from heaven, with a loud command,
with the voice of the archangel
and with the trumpet call of God,
and the dead in Christ will rise first.

After that, we who are still alive and are left
will be caught up together with them in the clouds
to meet the Lord in the air.
And so we will be with the Lord forever.
1 Thessalonians 4:14-17

During the End Times, God will come down from heaven Himself to claim us. This is called the rapture. All Christians who have previously died and those who are still alive will participate in this event together. Like Enoch, Christians will be caught up in the air. Can you even imagine?

Enoch was a prophet. Life was challenging for him. He lived during a time when sin and violence ruled the day and not many were righteous. Enoch lived a life of faith and was a bold witness to the Gospel and the upcoming judgment.

He boldly declared that God would come in judgment. He was desperate for the people to turn from their sins and repent. This was his prophesy:

> The Lord has come with
> many thousands of His holy ones,
> to execute judgment upon all, and to convict all
> the ungodly of all their ungodly deeds
> which they have done in an ungodly way,
> and of all the harsh things which
> ungodly sinners have spoken against Him.
> Jude 14b-15, NASB

Notice he uses the word, "ungodly" FOUR times in one verse. The evil that swarmed around him was always forefront on his mind. His message wasn't a popular one. He was referring to the judgment that will occur when Jesus Christ returns, leading the armies of heaven, condemning Satan, and judging with justice.[1]

Jesus will not send a famine or a flood. He will not send another in His place—not a messenger or even an angel. He will come Himself. He will execute judgment upon all people. No one will escape. Just as the flood destroyed all who were outside the ark, the final judgment will encompass all the ungodly. Justice will prevail at the hands of Jesus Christ, the only Judge. There will be no jury trial. No defense. Every mouth will be stopped.

No matter the darkness of our world or the pervasive prevalence of evil surging around us, we have the promise of our Lord's return to encourage and motivate us to live blameless and righteous lives.

So why did Enoch escape death? All we are told is that he walked with God and had great faith; the rest is unclear.

What does this mean for us? How are we to live? Micah gives us a glimpse into God's desire for us.

> And what does the LORD require of you?
> To act justly and to love mercy
> and to walk humbly with your God.
> Micah 6:8b

We are told God's desire is that we walk with Him—with humility. This isn't a suggestion, but a requirement. Walking with God is a process of unbroken fellowship as we commune with Him all day long, sharing life's ups and downs together. It is a lifestyle where we give God our focus and let go of distractions. We align our will with His, no matter the personal cost to us. We choose to glorify Him in every possible way, giving Him credit for victories and blessings and seeking His input during challenges. As we walk with God, we purposely reject the ways of the world.

If we are wise, we will seek to follow Enoch's example as those who walk faithfully with God. And one day, after we die, we too will be caught up in the air like Enoch and transported personally by our Lord directly to heaven to live for eternity with Jesus and all our loved ones (those who chose to live for Christ during their lives) who have gone on before.

---

[1] Revelation 19:11 – I saw heaven standing open and there before me was a white horse, whose rider is called Faithful and True. With justice he judges and wages war.

31

⁓

Count the Cost

oin me on a trip back in time to the year 30 A.D. Let's travel to Jericho, just outside the gates to the city. Something miraculous is about to take place. Let's peek in and take a look.

Jericho, one of the oldest inhabited cities in the world, was a wildly populated resort town about 15 miles northeast of Jerusalem—noisy, bustling, and bursting with activity. People flocked there to get away from the burdens of life. Many of the wealthy and powerful of the day, including royalty, built their winter palaces there, including King Herod the Great. Herod loved the climate, its mild winters, and the bountiful springs. Jericho was coined the "City of Palm Trees."[A]

Jericho, however, was a city of disparity. It catered to the rich and influential, yet it had its fair share of poverty. Homeless outcasts and the crippled often lined the streets outside the gates to the city because it was a great place to get handouts as the wealthy passed by.

This was an especially busy time, just before Passover. Many people were traveling by foot from their hometown, through Jericho, as they made their way to Jerusalem.

On this particular day, beside the road sat a blind man. His name was Bartimaeus. Sadly, blindness was a rather common condition of this time due to disease and unsanitary conditions. Most occupations of that day required physical labor. Since he was blind, Bartimaeus couldn't get a job to support himself, so he relied on handouts. There were no welfare programs, charities, or governmental programs to help him. So he was at the mercy of the generosity of others in order to survive.

Day after day, year after year, he sat beside the road and begged from those who passed by. One day Bartimaeus heard a commotion and was told that Jesus and His disciples were coming along the road. Jesus always made a point to visit Jericho on his trips to Jerusalem. Jesus was on His way to Jerusalem to celebrate Passover one last time before his trial and crucifixion. This would be Bartimaeus's last opportunity to reach Him. It was his only chance to change his life forever.

Bartimaeus, believing in Jesus and the power He had, cried out to him from a place of deep-seated desperation. Many reprimanded him and tried to silence him, but Bartimaeus, filled with hope, shouted all the more without regard to what others thought.

> Jesus, Son of David, have mercy on me!
> Mark 10:47

Jesus wasn't going to allow such a loud and persistent proclamation of faith to go unnoticed. When Jesus acknowledged him and called out to him, Bartimaeus jumped to his feet, threw aside his cloak, and went to where he was told Jesus was standing.

His cloak

Let's stop a moment and consider his cloak. This garment was like a coat, but without sleeves. Warm and thick, it was probably made from wool, fastening at the shoulders, and reaching to the ankles. Certainly it had pockets.[B] It provided protection from the cold, wind, and rain. Bartimaeus probably had it his whole life. In many ways, it was his comfort; but more than that, it was his identity. Perhaps it was the only thing of value he possessed. It almost certainly contained whatever coins people had given him as he begged. Yet when Jesus appeared, Bartimaeus eagerly tossed aside his identity to identify with Christ. His cloak seemed to be in his way that day.

His request

Jesus asked him, "What do you want me to do for you?"[1] Bartimaeus replied, "Rabbi, I want to see."[2]

Being aware of and naming his desire in Jesus's presence was the entry point to a new life in Christ. Bartimaeus was willing to become vulnerable by naming what he lacked. He emptied himself so that Jesus could fill him and meet his deepest need. Jesus healed him immediately and replied, "Your faith has healed you."[3]

How did Jesus know Bartimaeus had faith and was a believer? It was known that the Messiah would be a descendant of King David. By calling Jesus the Son of David, he showed that he recognized Jesus as the promised Messiah.

Bartimaeus had heard travelers, passing through, talk about the miracles Jesus performed—healing the lepers, the lame, and the demon-possessed—the dead made alive again. Everyone else referred to Jesus as teacher, rabbi, or even someone who could do magic. But Bartimaeus believed Jesus was much more than that: He knew Jesus was the Messiah prophesied in the Old Testament.

Bartimaeus walked by faith, not by sight! Although he had been blind physically, he had 20/20 spiritual vision. His faith brought the healing he so desperately desired. Although physically blind, his spiritual vision was far superior to that of the religious elite around him who were sighted. He received his physical sight that day—so his physical sight matched his spiritual sight. He then followed Jesus along the road, walking in his new life, likely serving Him with his gifts. (Please read the full story in Mark 10:46-52.)

What about us?

We, too, are surrounded by activity. Our schedules are jam packed. People are everywhere! We frantically fight the clock, running here and there, from one endeavor to the next. We get used to noisy restaurants, crowded stores, traffic jams, and people everywhere scurrying about without regard to courtesy or kindness. Yet way deep down, beneath the noise, the activity, and the busyness of our lives, there is a stirring of our soul. Perhaps you feel like Bartimaeus felt—overlooked, ignored, mistreated by life. It is here that God's Holy Spirit is already at work within us, helping us to recognize our deeply held spiritual desire.

Bartimaeus knew this opportunity would pass him by if he didn't act. If he didn't courageously call out to Jesus that day, he would have sat by the road begging until he died, doomed to a life of despair and darkness. This same opportunity lies before you today. Today may well be the greatest opportunity you will ever face.

Do you have a cloak? What part of your identity is in the way? What part of your comfort from the storms of life is becoming a hindrance? What do you need to throw off in order to fully come to Jesus and serve Him well?

Bartimaeus knew that when he tossed aside his cloak, anyone could take it and run off with it and he would not have the means to replace it. Yet, he felt it was necessary to take that risk as the cloak was keeping him from running to Jesus. You see, Bartimaeus knew that coming to Jesus is not without personal cost. Everyone who comes to Jesus and takes on His identity must give up something of value—perhaps family or friends, pleasure, or a stubborn habit or addiction they've been embracing. Don't be afraid of the cost. In the end, the sacrifice you make is minor compared to the cost of your soul.

What good is it for someone to gain
the whole world, yet forfeit their soul?
Or what can anyone give
in exchange for their soul?
Mark 8:36-37

Perhaps you have physical sight yet lack spiritual sight. Are you spiritually lost? Only Jesus can open your eyes and cure your blindness. Seek Him.[4] His Word promises you will find Him. If you aren't saved, you cannot afford to miss the offer of salvation through faith in Christ. Perhaps you are saved, yet you have a great spiritual need weighing heavily upon your soul. State your need for wholeness and spiritual healing. Jesus is asking you to name your greatest spiritual longing—a desire He placed deep within your soul.

God yearns to hear you call to him and when you do, it will delight Him! He hears sincere believers calling out to Him amidst a frenzied, chaotic world of non-believers simply making noise. He hears you amidst a cacophony of turmoil. He also hears the people who are trying to silence you with criticism and ridicule; He hopes you won't worry about what others think and give up.

Don't allow anything to keep you from Jesus, who loves you more than life itself—literally, as He gave up His life for you! He wants to save your soul. Get serious about seeking Him. Jesus is worth *any* price—*any* loss—*any* sacrifice. He is the only One worthy of your soul.

One day, the opportunity will be gone forever. Like Bartimaeus, it may be your last chance; you don't know what tomorrow will bring. What doors stand open for you right now that one day soon may be shut forever? If you aren't saved, you can't afford to miss the offer of salvation through faith in Christ. Perhaps you are saved, yet you have another pressing spiritual need. When He hears you calling out to Him, Jesus will stop dead in His tracks to listen to you. He has turned His attention to you.

He is asking you, "What do you want me to do for you?" He awaits your answer. Name your greatest spiritual desire and allow Jesus to make you whole. Once you define it, Jesus will help you order your life by it as you follow Him.

Don't be afraid to be vulnerable before Him. Name what you lack. Be willing to empty yourself so Jesus can fill you and meet your deepest need. Then walk in victory!

To God's glory!

---

[1] Mark 10: 51

[2] Mark 10:51b

[3] Mark 10:52a

[4] Jeremiah 29:13 - You will seek me and find me when you seek me with all your heart.

32

What Chariots Have You Surrounded?

*E*lisha was a great prophet to Israel. Because of insight he gained from the Lord, he was able to stop invasions of the Syrian Army as they sought to destroy Israel. Time after time, Elisha knew where the Syrian soldiers decided to set up camp for the night and he would notify Israel so that they could avoid them. The King of Syria became furious and tried to take Elisha out.

One morning Elisha's servant got up and beheld an alarming sight! He saw an enormous army had encircled the city, well-positioned to trap them. Struck with terror, he panicked and immediately ran to Elisha to inform him of the siege that would undoubtedly befall them!

When the servant of the man of God
got up and went out early the next morning,
an army with horses and chariots had surrounded the city.
"Oh, my Lord, what shall we do?" the servant asked.
2 Kings 6:15

Teeming with adrenaline and gripped with fear, the servant urgently looked to his master for a plan of escape. Elisha, filled with godly confidence and courage, looked at life through the eyes of faith. First, he reassured his servant. Then he prayed to the Lord for a godly perspective.

"Don't be afraid," the prophet answered.
"Those who are with us are more
than those who are with them."
And Elisha prayed,
"Open his eyes, LORD, so he may see."
2 Kings 6:16-17a

In His grace, the Lord responded.

Then the LORD opened the servant's eyes,
and he looked and saw the hills full of horses
and chariots of fire all around Elisha.
2 Kings 6:17b

Chariots of battle

What chariots have you surrounded? Are they chariots of despair and depression? Perhaps they are chariots of discouragement? Maybe your chariots are marked with anxiety and worry. Or possibly chariots of fear? Does it feel like they are closing in around you and holding you captive such that you can't escape? Do you feel trapped? Are you wringing your hands in despair like Elisha's servant, wondering, "What will I do?"

There's hope! God is so much greater than your depression and your anxieties. He is far more powerful than your discouragement and your fears. Ask Him to open your eyes so you can see His power and love working together to fight your battles. What you see in the physical realm isn't the whole picture. Don't be deceived by appearances. Appreciate the fact that there is always a spiritual reality we cannot see from a human perspective. Only God can fully see all that is occurring in the spiritual realm because He sees from a divine perspective. He is working in your life and on your behalf in ways you cannot see. Remembering that Truth exists—objective and fixed, not in flux with our emotions—will help you overcome your enemies:

- the ones that distort reality, filling you with fear and paralyzing you
- the ones that steal your joy and peace
- the ones that keep you from having the full life that Jesus promises

The horses and chariots that surround you aren't all that's out there! I promise. Place your faith in what is unseen because you know and trust God's promises to always be present, to fight for you, and to provide for you. God is exactly who He says He is. When you step out in holy confidence, your life of faith becomes visible evidence of an invisible truth.

If you could see things from God's divine perspective, you would see that God has His horses and chariots of fire all around your enemies. His strength and power are way more powerful than the enemies holding you hostage. His troops are blazing with fire, illuminating the battlefield, and exposing the evil with God's holy Truth. The darkness has fled. Your faith—even faith as tiny as a mustard seed[1]— penetrates the darkness and the darkness cannot overcome it.[2] Light is always victorious; evil will not prevail, regardless of how things may appear with our human eyes.

Don't allow worldly chariots to intimidate and threaten you. Stand strong, confident, mighty in His power. Know that God is *not* wringing His hands, saying, "Oh no! I didn't see *that* coming!" He has it covered! And His power is greater! Trust that He has a plan and it's for your good and His glory.

173

We all have faith in something. Our foundation of faith is anchored in the object of our faith. If the object of our faith is the living God of the Christian faith, it's crucial that we understand who He is and what Truths He stands for. This understanding comes from knowing what His Word says about Him.

As you read your Bible, ask God to open your eyes and illuminate His Truth for you to see it accurately. Then your fears, discouragement, anxieties, depression, despair, and doubt will subside because you will realize that His blazing chariots have achieved victory from that which oppresses you.

May God bless you, protect you, and illuminate His power and glorious victory in your life!

---

[1] Matthew 17:20b – Truly, I tell you, if you have faith as small as a mustard seed, you can say to this mountain, "Move from here to there," and it will move. Nothing will be impossible for you.

[2] John 1:5 – The light shines in the darkness, and the darkness has not overcome it.

33

On Fire

 candle has one purpose: to be lit so it can shine its light. A candle has a hole in the center specifically designed for the wick. Without the wick, it is just wax. It can't be a light. It doesn't function how it was designed to function.

My children and I used to make candles. We bought sheets of colored wax, then rolled them to make taper candles. You can also buy blocks of wax, then melt them in a double boiler. When it is 140 degrees, you pour it into molds and allow the wax to set as it cools. It is purposeless if you go to all this work and don't add the wick. What good is a chunk of wax?

But we may have a problem. What if I put the candle on the table, but never light the wick? It can only sit there and look pretty but without the flame, it still doesn't fulfill its purpose. Or I may light the candle for a while, but when I blow out the light, the darkness is free to reign once again.

We are like a candle

We have the same purpose: to be the light. We also have a hole in our center which has been specifically designed and shaped for God. When we accept Jesus Christ as our Lord and Savior, the Holy Spirit comes to live inside of us. Our *wick* is the Holy Spirit. Without the Holy Spirit as the divine light within, we can't shine; we're just darkness like the rest of the world. We can sit there and maybe look pretty, but we don't function like we were designed to function. We were designed to have a wick—the Holy Spirit.

We can light our fire

We, too, have the ability to shine the light of our faith in the dark world that surrounds us. But only if our *wick* is lit. God created us for the fire of the Holy Spirit. How do we light the fire of the Holy Spirit within us? There's only one way: by walking in the Spirit—in obedience.

Imagine going for a walk with a friend. You walk side by side and your strides match one another. No one walks in front; no one walks in back. If your friend is walking more quickly, you step up the pace. If your friend assumes a slower pace, your steps naturally slow down. You talk, you laugh, you share your thoughts. Imagine if your friend pulled out a harmonica and played it while you tried to talk. It's not only distracting, but inconsiderate.

When we walk in the Spirit, we are walking with God. This is a metaphor for daily living together, making consistent forward progress. It means we share life together, allowing Him to influence us—relying on His guidance and leadership.[A] It means we don't "play our harmonica" when He's talking, nor get distracted (by our ungodly habits, unhealthy relationships, entertainment, thoughts, etc.) when He is talking. We align our steps and our will with His. We don't rush ahead and we don't lag behind. We walk in step with Him. And when the watching world sees us, they know we have been walking with Jesus because we are different from the world. We have melded into the Person with whom we have been walking. When people look at us, they see Jesus.

We either walk in the Spirit (with God) or we walk in the ways of the world. We can't do both. We must make a choice.

The aroma of life

Candles are also aromatic; they bring pleasure as they release the scent contained within the wax. This reminds me of the incense that was burned in times of victory.

Warren Wiersbe describes how this played out in Bible days, "If a commander in chief won a complete victory over the enemy on foreign soil, and if he killed at least 5000 enemy soldiers and gained new territory for the emperor, then that commander in chief was entitled to a Roman Triumph."[B] It was the crowning achievement of his military career.

This Roman Triumph was a special processional of the Roman army—a parade of sorts—to honor the conquering commander and his soldiers. The victorious general entered the city sitting in a chariot pulled by four horses. He was preceded by the enemy captives and followed by his troops.[C]

Roman priests burned incense in the parade as a means of celebrating the conquering army. To the triumphant soldiers, it was a sweet scent that meant life and victory. What a festive day this was for the citizens of Rome!

But to the enemy soldiers and leaders who were forced to participate in this processional, it was a different story. They were being led to their death at the mercy of wild beasts so this fragrance meant death and defeat.[B]

Paul, having witnessed these processionals, uses beautiful imagery to make an important point.

Living for His *Glory*

Thanks be to God, who always leads us
in triumphal procession in Christ
and uses us to spread the aroma
of the knowledge of him everywhere.
For we are to God the aroma of Christ
among those who are being saved
and those who are perishing.
2 Corinthians 2:14-15

Paul likens believers who walk in unity with the Lord to the incense the Roman priests burned. As believers, we shine our divine light into the darkness around us, giving off a fragrance that people notice. This scent is pleasurable to believers and offensive to nonbelievers. To believers, we are the fragrance of Jesus Christ—of eternal life and victory. To nonbelievers, this fragrance is offensive as it is the scent of death and defeat.[1]

Of primary importance, however, is that this scent is pleasing to the Lord—a form of worship—as it rises to the heavens in majestic glory.

---

[1] 2 Corinthians 2:16a – To the one we are an aroma that brings death; to the other, an aroma that brings life.

34

❦

A Consuming Fire

My husband and I enjoy reading with a candle burning nearby. There's something about the flickering flame that brings peace and joy. As we explored in the last chapter, we are like a candle; our *wick* is the Holy Spirit in our core. Its flame flickers within us as it shines light in the darkness.

Before we leave the room, we blow out the candle. Can we symbolically blow out our wick—the light within—as well? No, not really, as the Spirit will always shine within us. But we can hide the light of the Holy Spirit so it isn't visible. We do this when we quench (or grieve) Him by giving into the temptation to sin. When our thoughts, attitudes, words, and/or actions are not righteous or honorable and we choose to follow our own selfish desires, it's like we put a basket over our light. Then when the world looks at us, they see us and not Christ. We do this when we lie, curse, steal, express our anger, are sexually immoral, get drunk or high, don't forgive, don't love others, etc.

It's important to remember that every sin is, first and foremost, against God.

Do not grieve the Holy Spirit of God,
with whom you were sealed
for the day of redemption.
Ephesians 4:30

Do not quench
the Spirit.
1 Thessalonians 5:19

This is called quenching (or grieving) the Spirit. Then
we invariably look for something else to fill up that void
inside—something worldly.

A consuming fire

Do you remember when Moses saw the fire in the
burning bush? It was most unusual because "though the
bush was on fire it did not burn up."[1]

Our family has done a lot of campfires. (We love
s'mores; what can I say?) Campfires always destroy and
burn up the wood—the object that feeds it. The bush that
Moses saw was flaming with fire, but the bush stayed intact.
This is because it was God's fire! God's fire consumed the
bush but didn't destroy it. God has been called, "a
consuming fire."[2] He created us to be on fire for Him with
the fire of the Holy Spirit within us. This holy fire is the *only*
fire that consumes us (permeates and fills up) without
destroying us.

There are many fires in this world. And worldly fires
always destroy. I'm wondering what fires you may be
feeding right now that are threatening to destroy you. We
are really good at fanning those initial sparks until they
quickly get out of control, aren't we? And sadly, we usually
don't even see it coming until we're in a mess. And it
doesn't take long until these worldly fires start to burn us
from the inside out.

God's fire, which burns within us, doesn't feed on us
(and hurt us) because God is self-existent. Instead, He tells
us to feed off of Him. His fire contains a power He invites

us to have. No other fiery passion will ever guard us from getting burned and offer us something new in the process.

What passions are burning within your soul? If the fire within you is not of God, you will either:

1. Get burned from feeding the fires of:
   - Selfishness/Pride
   - Busyness
   - Materialism
   - Anxiety
   - Fear
   - Approval seeking
   - Anger/Rage
   - Addictions
   - Unforgiveness
   - Bitterness
   - Power
   - Guilt
   - Greed
   - Lust
   - Insecurity
   - Envy
   - Popularity
   - Etc.

2. Eventually fizzle out
   No fire will last if it's not from God.

If their purpose or activity is of human origin,
it will fail. But if it is from God,
you will not be able to stop these men;
you will only find yourselves
fighting against God.
Acts 5:38b-39

Either we're on fire for God or we're just on fire. Let's make sure the fire that burns within us is from God and is Holy Spirit-driven! Then nothing will be able to stop us! To God be the glory! All victory is from Him!

---

[1] Exodus 3:2b
[2] Hebrews 12:29

35

Dealing with Sorrow

I was talking with a young man recently. From the outside looking in, he seems to have it all together. He has a couple of successful businesses, a sizable income, constant female attention, athletic prowess, and an active social life. Yet in a moment of vulnerability, he readily admitted that he is depressed and living with a deep sense of self-loathing. I was shocked.

He was soft-spoken, seemed anxious, and gazed downward. Our discussion had become uncomfortable. He admitted to me, "I have done so many bad things over the years. I'm afraid to tell you."

I replied to him, "There is no need to tell me anything. Tell God. Ask for forgiveness."

"I'm afraid to tell God."

"Don't you think God already knows?"

Do you ever feel this way? Desperately guilty? In deep despair? With low self-esteem? Ashamed and humiliated by something you've done? Keeping your sins to yourself is a good way to self-destruct. It will destroy you, bit by bit, eating you alive from within. Take them to the only One who can forgive them and wipe the slate clean. Then you can start over. In the Christian life, you get as many do-overs as you need.

Two ways to respond to sin

1) With worldly sorrow[1]
   - This comes from a posture of pride.
   - This expresses regret about the inconveniences of sin and/or resentment over the consequences one must suffer because of sin. (i.e.-We are sorry that we got caught.) This sorrow is manifested by turning inward toward oneself and away from God.
   - This leads to bitterness and misery.
   - The result: *bondage* in our sins. And regrets.
   - Ultimate result: Misery and *death*.
   - Example: Judas expressed worldly regret for betraying Jesus; he was overcome with despair, depression, and regret. He turned inward and away from God as he committed suicide.[2]

2) With godly sorrow[1]
   - This comes from posture of humility.
   - This expresses deep-seated grief or mourning for what one has done. This sorrow is manifested by turning toward God.
   - This leads to repentance, seeking forgiveness, and restoration—a changed heart. And ultimately peace and joy.
   - The result: *freedom* from our sins, healing, and changed behavior. No regrets.
   - Ultimate result: Relief and *life*.
   - Example: Peter expressed godly sorrow and repentance for disowning Jesus three times.[3] He turned toward God who then cleansed him of his

sin and shame. He went on to become a major leader in the church.

Go to Jesus. Name your sins and confess them with heart-felt, godly sorrow. God's grace is sufficient for every single sin you can think of. And then some!

Read this incredible promise from God.

If we confess our sins,
he is faithful and just and will forgive us our sins
and purify us from all unrighteousness.
1 John 1:9

When we approach Him with an attitude of repentance, asking to be forgiven, He cleanses us completely. No matter how many times we come to him. Just how extensive is this forgiveness? Take a look...

He has removed our sins as far from us
as the east is from the west.
Psalm 103:12, NLT

North and south are a finite distance apart because they end at the North and South Poles. East and west are infinitely spaced apart. You can go east or west forever.

Will repentance erase all the guilt you feel? Maybe not. Guilt is a natural human response. It serves as a warning to us not to repeat the sinful actions. But it should not control you and send you spiraling into an abyss of self-condemnation. In fact, until you fully understand the depth of the forgiveness God gives you, your guilt will not disappear. When you confess with a sincere heart, your sins are not just covered up, but erased completely. Forgiveness is a beautiful gift from a loving, compassionate Father. Receive it with gratitude, then move on. And sin no more.

Did my young friend go to God in repentance? He did not. He chose not to repent, thinking God would reject him. Choosing not to repent is an act of pride and keeps us from a right and healthy relationship with our Savior. God is reaching out to you in love.

A long time ago, a woman was caught in adultery. Old Testament Law commanded stoning for such an offense. Yet Jesus forgave her completely and extended love, not condemnation.[4] His parting words were, "Go now and leave your life of sin."[5]

Repentance has two parts

First, we confess our sin. Second, we turn from our life of sin and sin no more. If you are caught in a lifestyle of perpetual sin of the same nature, get out. Do whatever it takes. Leave it behind. Move out from living with your girlfriend. Pour the alcohol down the drain. Burn the Playboy magazines. Find new friends. Don't go into the casino or the bar; don't even drive past them. Set up your computer to lock you out of certain websites. Cut up the credit cards. Throw out the junk food. Do whatever it takes. It will be hard; it will take courage. But it will be worth it.

Paul understood as he struggled with sin.

> I don't understand why I act the way I do.
> I don't do what I know is right.
> I do the things I hate.
> Instead of doing what I know is right,
> I do wrong.
> Romans 7:15,19, CEV

It's the human condition. We all have a sinful nature, and we are vulnerable. We fight an inward struggle between sin and doing what's right. Thank God that we have been given another chance through His grace and mercy.

As believers, we have the Holy Spirit living inside us. Let the reality of Christ's power living in you lift you up to real victory over sin. This Spirit is the same Spirit that raised Jesus from the dead.[6] We aren't left to flounder about and struggle on our own. Praise God! Ask Him to grow your desire for Him and strengthen you in His grace for His glory. And ask Him for the courage to humbly repent. He will graciously provide all you need.

Then savor the taste of true freedom!

For His glory!

---

[1] 2 Corinthians 7:10 – Godly sorrow brings repentance that leads to salvation and leaves no regret, but worldly sorrow brings death.

[2] Matthew 27:3-5 – When Judas, who had betrayed him, saw that Jesus was condemned, he was seized with remorse and returned the thirty pieces of silver to the chief priests and the elders. "I have sinned," he said, "for I have betrayed innocent blood." "What is that to us?" they replied. "That's your responsibility." So Judas threw the money into the temple and left. Then he went away and hanged himself.

[3] Matthew 26:75 – [Peter] went outside and wept bitterly.

[4] Romans 8:1 – There is now no condemnation for those who are in Christ Jesus.

[5] John 8:11

[6] Romans 8:11a- The Spirit of him who raised Jesus from the dead is living in you.

36

~~

Set Free

What a mess! As I was driving to my daughter's home in Winston-Salem, North Carolina with our four small dogs, clouds darkened the sky, and a splattering rain quickly dotted the expressway. When we arrived, Rebecca was at work and since I couldn't get in her garage, I temporarily parked in the street, car idling, blinkers on, wipers running. Rain spilled down in sheets as I ran one of the dogs across the lawn and into her home. When I quickly returned for the others, I discovered that in their anxiety at being left behind, the other three dogs had locked me out of the car. Yes indeed, the little lock button was in the downward position—the key resting on the center console. They were trapped inside—helpless.

I darted back and forth, from one side of the car to the other, so that the dogs would follow me, and in their enthusiasm, possibly press on the unlock button with their little paws. No such luck. From side to side in the rain I repeatedly ran, doing all kinds of ridiculous gymnastics to keep them excited and moving. Needless to say, they got tired of this absurd game and eventually just followed me with their eyes, their feet no longer moving. I must have looked like a crazed idiot—drenched, frustrated, and exhausted. To make matters worse, I was in a hurry; I had an appointment an hour away and had planned to leave them in Rebecca's home while I was gone. And, as luck would have it, my cell phone was locked in the car with my key. I was in such a hurry to bolt through the rain, I had left both critical items behind.

As the rain lessened to a gentle drizzle, a couple of sympathetic neighbors came out (with umbrellas) to see what this fool was up to. One of them offered me her cell phone so I could call AAA. Of course, my membership number was locked in the car, but I was able to call my husband and get the number. As we waited for AAA to arrive, we conversed about trivialities within 15-20 feet of the car. I was only halfway paying attention, my ears on high alert, hoping I would hear the car unlock should one of the little rascals miraculously jump on the unlock button.

Then I heard it!

It was subtle, but the car definitely unlocked. I sprang into action and ran to the car to open the door before they could lock it again. Oh, what a sweet sound to my ears! My dogs were no longer trapped inside. I could hop in the car to continue with my plans, unhindered by my plight.

This is how I imagine God—busy answering prayers and interceding on behalf of all the believers in the world, fighting battles and holding together the universe. Yet, He keeps an ear highly tuned to hear prayers of repentance. And when he does, he enthusiastically springs into action to forgive, setting people free. No longer trapped by the confines of their sin. Liberated from the mess of their transgression. Released. Freed. The burden lifted.

If the Son sets you free,
you will be free indeed.
John 8:36

If you have unconfessed sin, you are bound to it; it holds you captive. God has an ear finely attuned to your voice, eagerly awaiting your repentant prayer so He can release you from its burden, freeing you to get on with your life, unhindered by the jaws of its savage grip on you. Do you want to know true unabashed freedom? God is waiting. Take care of it right now. Break out of the chains of bondage to live gloriously free in Christ. Then get on with your life—in the joy of your salvation.

37

~⌒~

Take Home the Win!

*D*uring the winter months, football rules the land! We enthusiastically watch the teams battle it out on the field. We cheer with the touchdowns; we wince with the injuries. Thankfully, most tackles aren't of much consequence because the players are decked out in the full regalia of their team. They are wearing protective gear so that their bodies are safeguarded when tackled. They would be foolish to play without every piece of their uniform securely in place.

The football uniform consists of various pieces of equipment including (but not necessarily limited to) a helmet, shoulder pads, shoes, thigh pads, knee pads, a mouthguard, and compression shorts.

When the shrill whistle pierces the air and the teams burst forth to command the field and take on their opponents, they are ready!

Friends, every single morning, the whistle blows as you get out of bed. You enter the playing field of our world—which is far more like a battlefield—and you must be on top of your game. The opposing team—the enemy—will do all they can to get the touchdown for their side by trying to bring you down. Expect to be tackled. Anticipate opposition as you execute a daring pass or kick the field goal. Defenders from the other team will be ready to try to intercept your best efforts.

The enemy is strategic. The opposing team has played and replayed all your past games ad nauseum; they have studied your strengths and know your best moves. They have analyzed your pockets of weakness. They know how to play defense and are particularly strong on offense.

What chance do you have? You and I have one hope; our hope is in our Coach. Thankfully, our Coach is confident and has the victory secured. But there is a game to be played to get us to the final buzzer. It's a competition unlike anything we can even imagine. We must keep our eyes on our Coach: our Coach is Jesus Christ.

The first thing our Coach does is provide us with a uniform—our protective gear. This is called the armor of God.[1] It's not the knock-off brand of armor at the local big box store. This is the actual, foolproof, divine armor of the living God. It is different from the uniform the football players wear. Our uniform protects our hearts and minds because it is spiritual armor, and it makes us able to stand our ground. Don't take this armor lightly.

If football players step onto the playing field without their uniform, their opponent will dominate. They will be at greater risk for injury and become a liability to their team.

If we step onto life's playing field without the full armor of God or are careless in its application, then our opponent—Satan—will try to push us all over the field; and he will probably be quite effective. We will be pawns in his hand. We will be at a greater risk for moral failure and will almost certainly become a liability to our team—the team of Christian saints.

Each morning, as you step out of bed, don the armor of God and secure it in place. Be aware of what's playing out in front of you each day. There's a battle of wills going on and the minutes are ticking down. Be on guard. When you courageously live your faith on the turf of your life, realize the opponents may send an all-out blitz to sack you or pressure you into throwing an incomplete pass.

Expect that some days you will only complete 50% of your passes due to an intense pass rush you couldn't avoid.

There may be taunting and trash talking. Ignore the chatter. There may be penalties. Keep playing.

Satan may make sure that as you run the play, it becomes a disaster. It may take the breath out of you. You aren't finished yet. You got this. Just keep pounding.

As you pass the ball to gain some ground, expect some players will try to intercept the pass. And as you run for the goal line, you may get hit from the blind side, the ball knocked loose for a forced fumble. Go for the recovery and keep possession. Don't give up.

Sometimes you need a handoff. Let your teammates (fellow Christians) help. Work together.

You may get tackled and that's ok; it's expected. Refuse to be defeated. Brush yourself off. Get back up. Another play awaits.

Friends, there's a lot at stake. The clock is ticking. We need to keep playing. It's up to you. Are you ready to get out there and play hard? Lives are at stake. The team is depending on you. Let's take home the win—for God's glory!

Game on!

Please read chapter 40 on the armor of God as a follow-up to this chapter.

---

[1] Ephesians 6:13 – Put on the full armor of God, so that when the day of evil comes, you may be able to stand your ground.

38

Battles

*A*mericans have fought in twelve major wars—on our own soil as well as abroad. The first four wars in our history (the Revolutionary War, the War of 1812, the Mexican-American War, and the American Civil War) were largely fought here on our home turf. War, no matter the reason, is always ugly—a grueling nightmare of one battle after another.

In those early wars, men of all ages were drafted or joined the cause. The minimum age to join the army was 18 years of age. Many young boys were eager to fight and lied about their age; tens of thousands joined much younger, some as young as 14 and 15.

The life of a soldier was a life of one challenge after another. Soldiers had to deal with hunger, malnutrition, inadequate clothing, isolation from families, inclement weather, frostbite, and even boredom between battles. Many of General Washington's men didn't even have shoes to wear in the freezing snow. With soldiers fighting in close proximity to one another in the trenches, infectious diseases such as dysentery and pneumonia were rampant. In some wars, cholera and typhoid fever were common and spread rapidly.

The soldiers were also victims of primitive medicine. Minor infections became deadly due to the lack of antibiotics. (Penicillin, the first true antibiotic, was first developed in 1928. But it wasn't widely available for another two decades.) War injuries and necessary amputations led to excruciating pain as knowledge of pain killers and anesthetics was minimal.

As a soldier, life was just—plain—hard!

- It was living on edge, waiting for the next attack which was inevitable.
- It was waiting for orders from the general.
- It was being prepared at all times—the uniform on, the weapon ready, the mind engaged.
- It was resting, when possible, to maintain strength for battle.
- It was living in constant stress, fear, exhaustion, anxiety, homesickness, and loneliness.

Such a sad time. I'm so thankful that was roughly 150 to 250 years ago. Things are much better now. Or are they?

Fast forward to today

I don't know if you've noticed, but we are in the midst of a very serious war too, but it's not a physical war. It's far more serious. It's a spiritual war—a war for our souls. It's lasting a long time—much longer than any of our other wars. And it's just as intense. Maybe more so.

Your enemy watches you very carefully; he is cunning and plans his attacks with precision based on intricate details of your life. Do you wish you could just move forward? Do you wish you could see the big picture from where you are? You can't. But there is a Commander in charge who does see the big picture—and He ranks higher than a general. He knows things you have no way of knowing. It's best to trust Him and follow His commands.

Ginny Dye has authored The Bregdan Chronicles, a brilliantly written, historical fiction series that encompasses the Civil War and Reconstruction. In the fifth book in the series, we see the power of the Union army overtaking the South through a series of intense and violent battles. In one scene, we get to peer into one of the trenches where two soldiers, fighting to end slavery, are talking. Clay, a 17-year-old boy, was battling discouragement.

> "We don't seem no closer than when we started," Clay said dubiously.
>
> That brought a chuckle from Moses [his superior]. "I'd say you're right. The one thing I know, though, is that we can't see the big picture from where we are. Grant and the generals know things we have no way of knowing. We have to trust them and follow their orders."
>
> "I reckon that be the truth," Clay said. He paused and stared out into the rapidly approaching darkness. "When you reckon the next orders be comin'?"
>
> "They'll come when they come," Moses responded. "The best thing you can do is get some rest. When they come, we'll have to be ready."[A]

What do your battles look like?

You, too, are waiting for direction and guidance. Moses's advice is spot on. No one knows when the orders will come. They'll come when they come. So you better get some rest. When your orders come, you'll have to be ready to move.

Rest—it's not inactivity. It's righteous activity. It's being still before God, eagerly anticipating and watching for His direction. It's praying. It's polishing up your sword (of the Spirit[1]) so that it is sharp and ready when you need it. When your Commander speaks, He will tell you when to move forward and where to go. Be ready.

There is no need to live in stress, fear, anxiety, and loneliness. If you have faith in your Commander, you can step into battle with confidence, knowing He goes before you[2] and will not be defeated. The battles ordained for you may be intense, but remember you aren't alone. He fights for those who trust in Him.[3] He fights for the faithful. and He gives blessings during the fight.

Don't be intimidated by the size of the enemy or the battle at hand. Let the power of your Commander dictate your confidence and trust. Some battles are quick and decisive. Some last a very long time, requiring you to persevere. Sometimes there is a break in the fighting, and you have a season of peace. But when the enemy assaults full force, you have no choice but to stand firm, ready to take on whatever is launched at you.

Each battle is a test of your faith. Don't give up! Your complete obedience will be rewarded—whether the fight be easy or hard. Be strong and courageous. Don't be afraid or discouraged. Your Commander has it under control. He is always with you and will help you every step of the way.[4] Ultimately our battles are for *our* good and for *His* glory. Keep your eyes on the One in charge! He is all you need.

The advantage we have is that we know the ultimate victory has already been won[5] despite the difficulty of the daily battles. The Israelites were assured the Promised Land; that victory was already secured. But they needed to fight many battles to claim that ultimate victory.[6,7] You, too, have also been assured of the victory, but there will be many battles you must fight in order to claim that victory. The victory ahead is so much more wonderful than you can imagine. If you could see the size of the blessings coming, now and on into eternity, you would better understand the magnitude of the battles you are fighting; but God hasn't given you that perspective. You can only trust Him and keep moving forward as He leads. The battles will come; don't be surprised when they do. And try not to complain. They are part of the divine plan.

So as you wait, be alert—listen for divine orders from above—step into the fray and fight courageously to the glory of God when called to do so, one step at a time. And don't stop until the job is done. Exciting times ahead; blessings and a beautiful victory await…

---

[1] Ephesians 6:17 – Take…the sword of the Spirit, which is the word of God.

[2] Deuteronomy 31:8 – The LORD himself goes before you and will be with you; he will never leave you nor forsake you. Do not be afraid; do not be discouraged.

[3] Joshua 23:10b – The LORD your God fights for you, just as he promised.

[4] Joshua 1:9 – Have I not commanded you? Be strong and courageous. Do not be afraid; do not be discouraged, for the LORD your God will be with you wherever you go.

[5] 1 John 5:4 – Everyone born of God overcomes the world. This is the victory that has overcome the world, even our faith.

[6] Psalm 60:12 – With God we will gain the victory, and he will trample down our enemies.

[7] 1 Corinthians 15:57 – Thanks be to God! He gives us the victory through our Lord Jesus Christ.

39

⁓

Fighting Giants

Satan will send many giants into our lives to attack all that we hold valuable. We mustn't sit back but rise up to fight. Let's explore the way David faced and defeated his giant, Goliath.

Points to consider when facing giants

- **Whatever your giants, they don't come at you just once.**

  They are relentless and badger you morning and evening, over and over. They don't give up. They threaten you across the gorge of your own personal valley of testing. Their goal is to intimidate, discourage, distract, and frighten you. David chose not to be intimidated by Goliath. He was defending God's honor. He didn't focus on the odds against him, but instead he remembered Whom he represented.

- **Trust only God.**

  Isaiah 26:3 states, "You keep him in perfect peace whose mind is stayed on you, because he trusts in you." Focus on your problems and you will be met with worry, insecurity, anxiety, guilt, discouragement, and/or fear. You will feel overwhelmed and defeated before the battle even begins! Focus on God and you will be met with hope, confidence, love, and gratitude; this all leads to perfect peace. A steadfast mind means a steady, unshakable, determined presence of thought. Real peace comes from trusting in the Lord. No matter what! In this verse, *keep* is a military term and means guarding as in protecting a fortress. As you trust God and maintain a steadfast focus on Him, God guards you mightily in His perfect peace.

- **Walk by faith, not by sight, focusing on God.**

If David walked by sight, he would have easily become filled with paralyzing fear. But he walked by faith and focused on defending God's honor. His focus changed the entire equation. Where is your focus? David's eyes weren't on the giant he could see; they were fixed on his God, whom he couldn't see. What battle are you facing? Cancer? Divorce? Loss of a job? Prodigal children? Addiction? Fix your eyes, not on this giant, but on God and your faith.

You may be too scared to face this battle. Or perhaps you decide to fight this battle, but without God—doing it your way in your own strength. If so, you're doomed to fail.

Do not focus on your giants. Obsessing on your troubles only causes them to grow in your mind far bigger than they actually are. As they appear bigger, you appear weaker, and God appears smaller. It's all a deception of the enemy. It's remarkable how often and easily we fall into this mindset.

Focus on God; do it His way, and He will equip you with His strength and wisdom to fight wisely. David's focus on God gave him the holy confidence to run forward into the attack without hesitation.

- ## Remember past victories and buck up your self-confidence.

   Charles R. Swindoll wisely observed, "So often, when facing our giants...we remember our defeats and forget our victories."[A] Not so with David. He recalled killing lions and bears who attacked his flock. These victories gave him the confidence necessary to charge forward with self-assurance and confront this new enemy head on in God's strength.

- ## Expect resistance.

   Whenever you step out in faith, there's always someone there to discourage you and possibly ridicule your plans. Many times, when you obey God, you may even get flak from your own family. They may misunderstand you and even accuse you unjustly.

   Expect this response and let it go. Focus instead on the fact that God is on your side, carrying you as you walk in faith to do the right thing.

- ## Fighting battles can be lonely and isolating.

   Your giants are yours alone. No other person can take your place and fight your battles for you. "It's on the lonely battlefield that you learn to trust God."[B] He is, after all, the only One who can help you. You can't face your giants effectively in your own strength.

- ## Confront your giants—your troubles—with confidence.

   David didn't run from trouble, but confronted it head on, with confidence, and at a full-out run.[1] Confrontation takes courage. Difficulties will not go away if you ignore them. They don't stay the same size either; they grow. If you tolerate or dismiss them, they will take over and consume you and your thoughts. Do not procrastinate. Confront your battle at the earliest opportunity before it grows into an alarming mountain of trouble!

- ## Never give up!

   Victory can be yours if you will walk in it and claim it. The battle may not be easy, but that's ok. God knows you can handle it with His support. Just don't quit. Keep praying. Keep seeking resolution. You might get hammered a time or two; just keep getting up.

   The next time Goliath threatens you, pull out your arsenal. He may retreat before you can even wind up to sling that stone.

- ## Deflect the honor.

   When victorious, always humbly deflect the glory to God for He is most worthy.

> Fear God and give him glory.
> Revelation 14:7a

The Book has been written

The ending is clear. Satan has already been defeated.

> The great dragon was hurled down—
> that ancient serpent called the devil, or Satan,
> who leads the whole world astray.
> He was hurled to the earth,
> and his angels with him.
> Revelation 12:9

> The God of peace will soon
> crush Satan under your feet.
> Romans 16:20a

If you have confessed your faith in Christ, He lives within you as the Holy Spirit! His unlimited power is available to you if you align your will with His and ask for His power to battle the challenges that Satan hurls your way. You don't fight alone—unless you choose to.

Follow David's example. Do not tolerate your giants. Do not run away, no matter how big they seem. Do not negotiate. Approach your battle from a position of God-given strength, not fear. Confront your battle with courage. Run—don't walk—toward the battle, unintimidated and boldly confident in Christ. Christ is the victor over Satan; as believers, we get to share in that victory with Him.

> With God we will gain the victory,
> and he will trample down our enemies.
> Psalm 60:12

> Thanks be to God!
> He gives us the victory through
> our Lord Jesus Christ.
> 1 Corinthians 15:57

> For everyone born of God is victorious
> *and* overcomes the world;
> and this is the victory that has conquered
> *and* overcome the world—
> our [continuing, persistent] faith
> [in Jesus the Son of God].
> 1 John 5:4, AMP

Run toward victory!
The battle is already won!
Thanks be to God!

———⚬———

Read Psalm 18; it is essentially the theme song for David's life. He wrote this psalm as a song to the Lord; it shows that the battle is God's, not ours alone.

---

[1] 1 Samuel 17:48

40

⤳

The Armor of God

*Y*ou are at war. It started the day you professed your faith in Jesus Christ. You can't choose whether or not you'll be in the war. You're in the thick of it, my friend. And so am I. Just as the Israelites were assured the Promised Land, they had to engage in many battles to claim it. So it is with us. We are assured a victory in the end, yet the battles to get there are real. This isn't a game. The enemy wants to destroy you—your life—those you love—your self-confidence. The battles are spiritual. And the battles are fierce.

War can be terrifying; I'm sure David was frightened plenty as he battled the enemy numerous times. But he chose to fight, not in His own strength which would have meant sure defeat, but in the strength of His Lord. He knew a vital truth: battling in God's power was far superior to the strength of any enemy.[1]

As battles rage, you have a decision to make. Will you be a warrior and fight? Being a pacifist won't cut it; the enemy won't back down. You are a child of the King of kings; royalty and victory are in your blood. Receive it by faith and step forward in bold confidence. God calls us to be mighty warriors in spiritual battles. Be alert and courageous; resolve not to get distracted.

Thankfully, God has this covered. He provides us with HIS very own armor—the armor of God. Weapons of this world are worthless in spiritual battles. We must use spiritual weapons, trusting God heart and soul, and follow His lead. Christ tells us that in order to stand strong in the power of the Lord, we must:

> put on the full armor of God,
> so that you can take your stand
> against the devil's schemes.
> Ephesians 6:11

To be victorious, we must suit up to fight effectively. In describing the six pieces of God's armor, Paul knew the people were accustomed to seeing Roman soldiers in full uniform. They would have certainly understood these metaphors, although much of the meaning is lost on us today. We will rectify that by the end of this chapter.

We cannot put on some pieces of the armor one day and other pieces another day; that leaves us too vulnerable. We need each piece every single day—the FULL armor of God. Let's briefly go through each one.

The Belt of Truth

> **Stand firm then, with the belt of truth**
> **buckled around your waist.**
> **Ephesians 6:14a**

The physical armor

The belt of the Roman soldiers was thick and heavy, about 2½ inches wide.[A] It was made of bronze plates connected with leather[B] and fitted with loops or buckles. When a soldier was ready for battle, he cinched his belt tight, as it was the foundation for all the rest. A secure belt supported and strengthened the soldier's core and secured other pieces of the armor. The breastplate was anchored onto the belt and the sword hung in the sheath, attached to the belt. If the belt became loose, the breastplate and sword became unsecured, and the soldier was left vulnerable to defeat.

The spiritual armor

God's Truth is the foundation for spiritual battle. The other pieces of our spiritual armor are anchored to it and dependent upon it. God's Truth, secured properly, strengthens our core, and flows through us, strengthening all areas of our life. It allows us to stand strong in battle, not falling victim to deceptions.

Satan, the father of lies,[2] will always try to deceive us. We disarm his tactics and impact by:

- Knowing God's Truth
- Walking in God's truth
- Aligning our life with God's Truth

If we expose everything to the light of His Truth and stand firm in the integrity of His Word, we can discern Truth and see the battle clearly. Our core is strengthened with His Truth and divine strength flows through us into all areas of our life. We are far less likely to fall victim to Satan's ploys and get hurt.

Without a reliable, sturdy belt, there will be disaster. A belt with a segment missing won't function properly; it must be one continuous, unbroken piece. As such, we must believe all of God's Truth—the whole Bible—or the belt falls apart, the breastplate slips off, and the sword falls out.

It's crucial all God's warriors get this right.

The Breastplate of Righteousness

**With the breastplate of
righteousness in place.
Ephesians 6:14b**

The physical armor

The breastplate securely fastened onto and was supported by the belt. It was made from two pieces of either leather, iron, or bronze sewn together.[B,C] It covered the body from the neck to the waist, front and back, with rounded pieces protecting the shoulders. It sported overlapping pieces of metal,[C] which allowed for flexibility of movement. The front and back sections tied together with leather.[B] The breastplate guarded the heart, lungs, and vital organs.

The spiritual armor

Our spiritual breastplate is made of the righteousness of Christ which He credits to us. Putting on His righteousness (aligning our lives with God's standards) protects our hearts from Satan's attacks. It guards our emotions so that we don't react based on our feelings, but on God's unchanging Truths.

If we start to believe that our own righteousness, effort, or good works can make us worthy of God's protection, our breastplate will fail, and we will lose the battle.

The Gospel of Peace

**And with your feet fitted with the readiness
that comes from the gospel of peace.
Ephesians 6:15**

212

The physical armor

Roman soldiers wore sandals or boots made with "thick leather soles studded with cleats of iron"[D] which helped them hold their ground in battle. In warfare, enemies would place dangerous obstacles in the path of advancing soldiers. The cleats allowed the soldiers to walk swiftly on treacherous terrain without injury.

Proper footwear saved many lives. They also provided traction. In hand-to-hand combat, blood quickly drenched the ground, becoming very slippery. Properly cleated sandals or boots were vital to making quick turns and running with confidence and sure footing.[A]

The spiritual armor

In spiritual battles, we must anchor our feet in the bedrock of Jesus Christ and the peace that comes through a relationship with Him. This gospel of peace allows us to traverse the otherwise painful trials of life without injury knowing that what awaits us eternally is far greater than anything we could possibly suffer in this world.

Readiness means being prepared to share the gospel of Jesus's life, death, and resurrection at any time. Jesus's work on the cross brings us eternal peace with God which gives us the confidence to fight with boldness.

Satan wants us to lose ground in our spiritual walk; he tries to get us to lose our balance and slip in our faith. He sets traps to trip us up. Solid footing allows us to stand strong against Satan's attacks as we seek to be peacemakers in all our interactions. We cannot survive the storms of life without God's peace anchored into every step we take. It offers stability and sanity in a world in which Satan tries to stir up discord, causing worry, anxiety, and fear. In His shoes, we can battle well without losing our footing.

The Shield of Faith

**Take up the shield of faith,
with which you can extinguish
all the flaming arrows of the evil one.
Ephesians 6:16**

The physical armor

The soldier's shield, also called the *scutum*, was large and heavy, made of wood and weighing over 20 pounds. It was nearly four feet tall and about 30 inches wide. The shield was not flat, but curved so a soldier could hide behind it easily.[E] It covered about three quarters of a man's body.[F]

The shield was primarily used as individual protection but could be lined up with others to form a large wall of protection in front of many soldiers as well as above them.

The opposing army often fired arrows flaming with fire, producing fear, insecurity, anxiety, intimidation, and chaos. The enemy tried to set soldiers on fire or the ground behind them, so attention was drawn to putting out the fire, rather than dealing with the warfare and enemy advances in front of them. This was a wildly effective tactic.

The shield also served as an emergency stretcher for the dead and wounded on the battlefield.[F]

The spiritual armor

Fiery trials are all around us. The enemy sends fiery arrows into our life all the time. He wants us so busy putting out internal fires that we have no time or energy to deal with the warfare around us, nor to be strategic in planning our own offensive moves.

Our faith, firmly rooted in God and His Word, is our shield—our defense against the fiery darts of the enemy:

doubt, deceit, depression, discouragement, and despair. Paul tells us to hide ourselves in Christ in faith.

Dr. Tony Evans uses a clever definition: "Faith is acting like it is so, even when it's not so, so that it might be so, just because God said so."

The shield is only effective if it is raised. This requires that we live in a state of readiness. We can either succumb to what we see or trust God with what we cannot see as we step out in faith, raising our shield when under attack. This activates our faith. David refers to this piece of armor as God's shield of victory.[3]

Raising the shield of our feelings, the shield of our own ideas, the shield of our own strategy, or the shield of our emotions will not extinguish the destructive arrows of our enemy. Holding our faith in front of us will deflect all Satan's darts, rendering them useless so that we can be effective for God. When we are walking by faith, God will instill a holy confidence in our steps.

The Helmet of Salvation

Take the helmet of salvation.
Ephesians 6:17a

The physical armor

In his listing of the armament, Paul's statement about the helmet is the shortest description given to any of the pieces. This is probably because it is straightforward; not much explanation is needed.

When suiting up for battle, the helmet was the last piece of the armor to be secured in place.[G] Usually made of bronze, the soldier's helmet fit securely with protrusions hinged on each side to cover the cheeks and jaws, offering protection against blows to the face. The helmet sported leather straps under the chin.[B] Poorer soldiers, unable to afford an all-metal helmet, would have had one made from leather with metal reinforcements.[G] Some had ear protectors riveted in place[A] and some had a metal piece in the back as a safeguard for the neck.[G]

The spiritual armor

Our spiritual helmet is our identity in Christ. As His heirs, our spiritual inheritance is salvation. This salvation refers to deliverance from sin and the power of sin as well as eternal salvation for our souls.

Jesus is our salvation; we cannot save ourselves. Our helmet protects the seat of our mind from accepting false doctrine and yielding to Satan's taunts and temptations. When properly secured, the helmet of salvation helps block toxic thought patterns that could become strongholds that control us. Replacing them with God's thoughts through His Word renews and restores our minds to a state of wholeness and strength in God. Not wearing the helmet in battle is dangerous. It leaves us vulnerable to Satan's deadly attacks, with our mind exposed and unprotected.

Walking in our salvation is liberating as our mind is protected and our thoughts are edifying and uplifting. It helps us reject worry, anxiety, and fear as we battle in confidence.

The Sword of the Spirit

**And the sword of the Spirit,
which is the word of God.
Ephesians 6:17b**

The physical armor

The sword of the soldier was double-edged and about 24-30 inches long, weighing roughly 3-1/2 pounds[A]; it was used for close combat. It sported a very sharp tip. Hung securely from the belt, it was handy at all times.

The spiritual armor

The sword, our only offensive weapon, is the Word of God—the Bible. I like Billy Graham's observation. "To the Christian, the Bible is not just a holy book to be placed on the shelf. It is a mighty weapon to be taken hold of with both hands and used in defeating the enemy."[H]

Our dear friend Tim, a former pastor and missionary, has lost enough of his vision from macular degeneration that he can no longer read his Bible. Yet he faithfully carries it to church with him. His rationale: "I don't want to be without my sword."

Jesus perfectly demonstrated the use of this powerful weapon during his 40-day wilderness challenge with Satan at the start of His ministry.[4] This is the same sword the Holy Spirit uses in the heavenlies to battle on our behalf. When we're being attacked, the Holy Spirit hands us His sword to use (as Bible verses and truths come to mind) when Satan is in our face with his evil schemes.

Satan would be delighted if we always kept our sword in its sheath, never drawing it out for battle, because he knows the amazing power and authority it contains. It's important to keep our spiritual sword sharp by knowing God's Word so we can wield it with bold confidence when challenged. When the enemy attacks us with fear, temptation, doubt, or anxiety or when he brings up past sins, we will be ready if we have our sword.

Prayer

**And pray in the Spirit
on all occasions.
Ephesians 6:18a**

All opposition from the enemy contains spiritual power. Fighting in the Holy Spirit through prayer is essential before we will experience victories. Jesus prayed on all occasions—earnestly, faithfully, and consistently. And He continues to pray for us as He is seated in heaven.[5] We would be wise to do the same by remaining alert and praying to Him about everything.

In spiritual battles, we are either advancing or retreating—winning or losing. We must fight to win by strapping on His armor every day for victory.

When the battle begins...

When the enemy looms large and you feel like you're going under, call out to the Lord in prayer, knowing your cry will reach His ears immediately and He will respond. He will rise up to defend you and equip you for battle. If we dare to take on the enemy in our own strength, he will chew us up and spit us out which is why God makes His armor available to us. When worn properly, we will be safe. The closer we abide with Him, the safer we are. Settle for nothing less than victory!

- God will cinch the Belt of Truth firmly around your core so you can stand firm in the integrity of His Word and resist Satan's devious and dangerous ploys.

- As you put on His breastplate of righteousness, God will protect your heart against enemy attacks as you respond with God's Truths, rather than emotions.
- With His spiritual footwear properly secured, He will make you spiritually agile so you can adapt to sudden changes in the enemy's offense and walk self-assuredly on uneven, dangerous terrain with courage.
- He will give you the strength to raise His shield of faith with reverence, honor, and bold confidence.
- With the helmet firmly in place, God will protect your mind so you can reject anxiety and fear as you walk with dignity in your sure salvation.
- As you read and study God's Word, He will help you keep your sword sharp and give you the courage to wield it with conviction when needed.

God will use every aspect of your battle for your good and for His glory. Suit up. The victory is yours.

---

[1] 1 John 4:4b – The one who is in you is greater than the one who is in the world.

[2] John 8:44

[3] Psalm 18:35

[4] Matthew 4:1-11 and Luke 4:1-13

[5] Romans 8:34 – Christ Jesus…who was raised to life—is at the right hand of God and is also interceding for us.

41

~∽~

A Holy Fruit Basket

*J*esus loved to teach using examples in nature.

> I am the vine, you are the branches.
> Those who abide in me and I in them
> bear much fruit,
> because apart from me you can do nothing.
> John 15:5, NRSV

When the Bible tells us something, we best listen. When it tells us twice, we realize it's especially important. But in seven short verses,[1] wrapped within the branches of a grapevine, Jesus tells us to abide ten times! It must be extremely important.

Our relationship with Jesus is like that of a branch to a vine. A branch is entirely dependent upon a vine; it cannot exist without the vine.

Jesus is the vine and we are the branches. What joy to see a vine bearing fruit on its tender branches! Jesus tells us that He chose us and appointed us (as the branches) "to go and bear fruit—fruit that will last!"[2]

When we put our faith in Jesus, God sends the Holy Spirit to live inside us. As sap flows through a vine to grow fruit, the Holy Spirit is the spiritual sap that flows through us to produce spiritual fruit. Just as "No branch can bear [physical] fruit by itself,"[3] we can't bear spiritual fruit by ourselves, but must remain on God's vine to do so.

It takes time and patience to grow fruit. When we try to rush the ripening process, the fruit isn't as flavorful as fruit allowed to ripen on its own. If you've eaten tomatoes in the winter that have been artificially ripened to speed up the process, you know they aren't nearly as good as a naturally, vine-ripened tomato in the summer. It takes time.

If we want to grow spiritually, we must sink our roots deep into a consistent relationship with God, staking our life on the gospel and extending the love of Christ to those around us. That's what we call abiding.

When we come to faith and abide in Christ, the outpouring begins as the Holy Spirit flows from Him through us, causing us to be more like Jesus as we produce spiritual fruit.

Spiritual fruit

Paul lists the spiritual fruit that God grows in us, as believers. There are nine: "love, joy, peace, patience, kindness, goodness, faithfulness, gentleness, and self-control."[4] These are all character traits of Jesus. To have the fruit of the Spirit is to be like Jesus.

- **The first fruit is love.** God is a God of love. That is the essence of who He is.
- **The next fruit is joy**. Joy flows directly from God's love.
- **Peace occurs** naturally—the 3rd fruit—when we have love and joy.
- And so it continues…

We can't see the fruit-making process as it occurs—inside the branches of the vine. In our lives, the spiritual fruit-making is also unseen. However, we often feel gentle nudging from the Holy Spirit which guides, strengthens, and transforms us as we become more like Jesus.

As we grow spiritually, we:

- pray for God's love and grace to drench us, watering and nourishing us.
- get on our hands and knees and till the soil of our heart with prayer to make it more receptive to seeds of growth.
- prune away bad habits when necessary.
- pray the cold and frost of harsh seasons aren't too much for us to bear.
- be thankful and delighted when an abundance of good fruit appears. A holy fruit basket!

As Christians, we can feel joy despite our circumstances because we choose to trust God, knowing He is aware of all things and is working behind the scenes. When our lives are intertwined with His, we can be assured that He will help us walk through adversity and suffering without sinking into debilitating lows. We know something good is going to come from the pain—the suffering—the trials. We don't worry like the world does because we know God is in control.

By their fruits...

Jesus tells us, "By their fruits you will know them."[5] People can tell if we're Christians by our spiritual fruit. They watch carefully to see if we have:

- **Love** instead of hatred, bitterness, or prejudice
- **Joy** instead of constant gloom
- **Peace** instead of turmoil and endless, crippling anxiety
- **Patience** instead of impulsive reactions
- **Kindness and goodness** instead of uncaring insensitivity and lack of compassion
- **Faith** instead of constant worry
- **Gentleness** instead of brashness and a short temper
- **Self-control** instead of acting as victims of our passions, using offensive language, or gossiping.

Inside out

No one can produce these qualities in himself. Trying harder to be godly won't work. Trying harder to have peace won't work. Nor joy. When we submit to God, only then will the Spirit be free to produce fruit that remains, even in our darkest days. In *The Cost of Discipleship,* Dietrich Bonhoeffer asserts,

> Fruit is always the miraculous, the created; it is never the result of willing, but always a growth. The fruit of the Spirit is a gift of God and only He can produce it. They who bear it know as little about it as the tree knows of its fruit. They know only the power of Him on whom their life depends.[A]

The Holy Spirit grows the fruit from the inside out. If we say, "I'm going to be more joyful," it's like tying oranges on a eucalyptus tree and calling it an orange tree. Fruit can only come from the inside—not the outside. Likewise, spiritual fruit results from the Spirit living inside us and through us. We can't grow our own fruit. That's why it's impossible to simply decide to be joyful. We can't just "choose joy" as is commonly espoused these days. Joy is a fruit of the Spirit and like all fruits, it must be grown from within. We can choose simple happiness, but not joy.

In *Surprised by Joy*, C.S. Lewis disclosed the story of his conversion from atheism to belief in God. The joy that came from his newfound faith surprised him as he came to trust in God. He wrote, "Joy is never in our power and pleasure often is."[B] Joy, like the other eight fruits, is a gift grown on the inside that blossoms and radiates on the outside when we come to faith and abide in Him.

It's really quite simple

We are a branch. A branch's job is threefold:

1) Grow.
2) Hang on through harsh winds and frightening storms.
3) Produce fruit.

A branch has no life without the vine. We may wonder how God grows and matures these fruits. He allows us to experience circumstances or trials in which we're inclined to express the exact opposite character trait. If we pray for peace, for example, we are likely to get trials that test our patience and try our soul. This way we learn to relax and trust God instead of becoming anxious. If we pray for joy, we're likely to experience situations that tempt us toward self-pity.

We must stay close to God and live in such a close relationship with Christ that our spirit is in tune with His. As He conforms us to His image, we are transformed through Him. We know we're abiding when we obey out of love, rather than duty. The closer we abide with God, the greater the quality and quantity of the fruit we produce—and the greater our desire to bear eternal fruit for the Kingdom as we bless and love others.

Look around! Be a fruit inspector. What fruit can you identify on people around you? What fruit can people see when they watch you?

> This is to my Father's glory,
> that you bear much fruit.
> John 15:8a

The more fruit we display in our lives, the more we glorify God. And the richer our lives will be!

---

[1] John 15:4-10, ESV
[2] John 15:16
[3] John 15:4, NLT
[4] Galatians 5:22-23, ESV
[5] Matthew 7:20, NKJV

42

The Wellspring of Life

Trees bear fruit from that which is contained within. Spiritually speaking, whatever fruit we produce is a reflection of what resides within our hearts.[1] The heart refers to the inner soul of a person; it is the seat of emotions and free will.

Some Bible versions say the heart is the wellspring of life. And indeed, it is! The heart is a delicate organ. It is like a spring that bubbles up from the inside and whatever is contained within splashes to the surface and spills over into thoughts. These thoughts become words and actions—essentially fruit from our hearts. These words and actions chart the direction our lives will take and therefore determine the person we will become. Most importantly, the content of our hearts ultimately determines the legacy we leave the world when we die. Therefore it is critical that we guard our hearts.

> Above all else, guard your heart,
> for everything you do flows from it.
> Proverbs 4:23

"Every good tree bears good fruit;" likewise, bad trees produce bad fruit.[2] Thieves steal, liars lie, rapists rape, murderers take lives, and adulterers cheat on their spouses because those sins are being produced from evil hearts. Evil hearts produce bad fruit. Matthew warns us to be wary of others because many people pretend to be gentle, good-humored sheep, but deep down, "they are ferocious wolves."[3] He advises us to study the fruit of other people in order to discern who they are. We aren't to be judges, but fruit inspectors. Jesus assures us, "By their fruit, you will recognize them."[4]

When we repent of our sins and receive Jesus as our Savior, He gives us a brand-new heart and a new spirit[5] which will produce new and different fruit for others to see. When we choose Him and His truths over the lies of the enemy, amazing things happen. Instead of bearing the fruit of bitterness, complaining, gossip, rage, anger, lying, envy, pride, etc., our fruit will now be of the Holy Spirit living in us. We won't be perfect, but with a heart submitted to our Savior, we will bear mostly good fruit: kindness, love, peace, gentleness, patience, self-control, compassion, and joy. We will offer grace and forgiveness as the rule, not the exception. The internal changes naturally transform the external in a visible and tangible way.

We can also influence the growth and conditioning of our heart in a positive, healthy manner by being careful what we watch and read, cautious about where we go, prudent in selecting the media we consume, and wise in choosing friends.

We will still sin and may go through a period of bearing little or poor fruit, but those who are abiding in Christ will not live a lifestyle of continual bad fruit. The transformation we undergo at the point of salvation is a radical transformation of our soul—a spiritual rebirth. As proof of that transformation, we produce good spiritual fruit—evidence of our genuine faith—to the glory of God.

If we profess the Christian faith, we must be certain that fellow fruit-inspectors see our fruit which disclose Christ's identity. I pray our fruit doesn't dishonor our Lord, but instead glorifies and magnifies Him.

---

[1] Mark 7:21-22

[2] Matthew 7:17

[3] Matthew 7:15

[4] Matthew 7:16a

[5] Ezekiel 11:19 - I will give them an undivided heart and put a new spirit in them; I will remove from them their heart of stone and give them a heart of flesh.

43

The Swab Test

Two years ago, I flew with my mother-in-law from Phoenix to Charlotte. She was coming to live here. At 89, she had advanced dementia and the mental status of a two-year-old. Well, wouldn't you know it—as we went through security, she was randomly chosen to have the TSA swab test…and failed. This test checks for chemicals that terrorists might use to make explosives: nitrates and glycerin.[A] She tested positive for nitrates.

Three men descended upon us in rapid fashion. There she sat, wide-eyed with apprehension and nervousness. She remained in a wheelchair holding her baby doll, unable to comprehend what was transpiring. One man took the baby doll; another grabbed her walker and cane. A particularly stern-looking official took her carry-on bag and marched across the way to a separate area. I was left behind with her looking confused and forlorn.

I wheeled her to the man who had the carry-on bag. With a very serious and professional demeanor, he donned latex gloves and hoisted the small suitcase onto a table. He unzipped the front compartment. He poised his hand over the space, then stopped, looked at me with a very somber face and said, "I'm going in…I don't know what I'm going to find." I calmly replied, "a plastic trash bag." He looked surprised and rooted around, pulling out the trash bag I had placed there from our local grocery store. He repeated the process with the next compartment. "I'm going in…I don't know what I'm going to find," to which I replied, "a couple of Depends." He looked startled, then I added, "Don't worry; they're clean." He looked surprised and tried unsuccessfully to keep a straight face. He proceeded to root around for a little bit, but the yield was less than exciting.

How very like our world

As we live our lives, we are on a spiritual battlefield and are called to infiltrate our world. We aren't to isolate, but to get involved with the messiness of life. Our Captain (Jesus) stands in control and sends us forward. We can trust Him.

Every single day, we can say, "I'm going in…I don't know what I'm going to find." And that's the truth; we don't! But our Captain does. And he gives us more than a latex glove. We have the full armor of God![1] (Please find more on the armor of God in chapter 40.)

It might get messy. It might get chaotic. We never know. But we are the soldiers of God's army, and we are told to advance and be ready for whatever we may find.

Dangers of bacon

I later discovered the reason the swab of her hands may have been positive. I had given her bacon to eat that morning for breakfast. She held it in her hand as she fed herself. Bacon has nitrates. So do hot dogs, sausages, ham, salami, corned beef, Vienna sausages, smoked salmon, jerky, and spinach. Just a warning: if you're flying, keep this little tidbit in mind!

44

Dealing with Anger

*A*nger and rage are escalating rapidly in today's culture. We see it everywhere: when driving, on social media, at the polling booths, in stores, at work, on college campuses, etc. We all have emotions and in this broken world with sinful people, there will be things that infuriate us. But anger isn't sinful; what we do with our anger—that's what *can* be sinful.

Joseph was one of 13 children; he had 11 brothers and at least one sister. His father, Jacob, loved Joseph the most. Sadly, this was a multi-generational problem; his dad favored Jacob's twin, Esau, yet Jacob was his mom's favorite.

Jacob openly expressed his favoritism toward Joseph and even gave him a richly ornamented robe as a symbol of his love. Joseph's response didn't help matters when he became conceited. He had two dreams where his brothers bowed down to him and served him, but he made the mistake of sharing these dreams with them which didn't set well. They reacted with anger and hatred which only spiraled out of control.

One day they seized him, tore off his coat, and threw him into a large cistern, intending to kill him. But just then, along came a camel caravan carrying spices and perfumes to Egypt. Judah convinced his brothers to sell Joseph into slavery instead, intending that he would live a very tough life of hard labor. Then they faked his death to their own father.[2] So much deception.

What went wrong?

Anger is an involuntary emotion of passion. When angry, we are on dangerous ground. Left unchecked, it can easily consume and control us, taking on a life of its own. It wields destructive power. We must not allow it to spill over into sinful actions. The damage we cause in our anger can be far-reaching and, in many cases, permanent. Many of us have lost our temper and we know the devastation we feel afterwards. And all of us have been victims of an angry outburst; we know how hurtful and upsetting that feels.

When Satan sees our vulnerability as our anger intensifies, this gives him traction[3] to do his thing: steal, kill, and destroy.[4]

- **Steal** our joy, peace, patience, and self-control.
- **Kill** the person's good name, their confidence, self-esteem, or character.
- **Destroy** a relationship, our integrity, and maybe far worse.

Anger is usually a response to underlying fear, jealousy, or being wronged. It is an outplaying of our sinful nature— our flesh—a result of our lack of self-control.

Those who live according to the flesh
have their minds set on what that the flesh desires;
but those who live in accordance with the Spirit
have their minds set on what the Spirit desires.
Romans 8:5

We have a choice

We have free will to choose how to live, whether it be by our own human nature and emotions or by the Holy Spirit's nature within us. If we choose to center our lives on God, submit to the Holy Spirit, and live by biblical standards, our life will be ruled by life and peace.[5] And anger won't get a foothold.

But if we choose to be controlled by our sinful nature and the things of this world, our anger will take over which leads to death, destruction, and chaos. The outcome is never good.

We can't choose both; the Holy Spirit cannot rule our life if emotions are already in charge and wielding control.

> You are not controlled by your sinful nature.
> You are controlled by the Spirit,
> if you have the Spirit of God living in you.
> Romans 8:9a, NLT

God knows our tendencies and has issued warnings in Scripture; He knows Satan will fully take advantage of our anger.

> In your anger, do not sin.
> Ephesians 4:26a

> Refrain from anger
> and turn from wrath.
> Psalm 37:8

And we can turn from that anger as we submit to the Holy Spirit.

It could have been avoided

Joseph's brothers reacted in their anger based on their impulsive, volatile, irresponsible, sinful nature and their unpredictable and every-changing emotions. If they had prayed to God and yielded to Him *before* acting, the outcome would have been very different. The Holy Spirit would have diffused the anger and Joseph would have experienced God's love, patience, and grace. Things would not have gotten out of hand. The brothers would have extended forgiveness and the relationships would have been restored.[6]

Paul issues this warning to fellow Christians.

As God's chosen people, holy and dearly loved,
clothe yourselves with compassion, kindness,
humility, gentleness and patience.

Bear with each other and forgive one another
if any of you has a grievance against someone.
Forgive as the Lord forgave you.

And over all these virtues, put on love,
which binds them all together in perfect unity.
Let the peace of Christ rule in your hearts.
Colossians 3:12-15a

We *will* get angry. We must decide today how we will respond when it happens. Will we choose life and peace? Or will we choose destruction and pandemonium? God has provided an out for us. We can choose to yield to the Holy Spirit and trust His power to overcome the desire to sin in our anger. I pray we will be wise enough to submit to Him at the next opportunity.

[1]Ephesians 6:11-17

[2] Genesis 37:12-35

[3] Ephesians 4:27 – Do not give the devil a foothold.

[4] John 10:10 – The thief [Satan] comes only to steal and kill and destroy; I have come that they may have life, and have it to the full.

[5] Romans 8:6 – The mind governed by the flesh is death, but the mind governed by the Spirit is life and peace.

[6] Ephesians 4:31-32 - Get rid of all bitterness, rage, and anger, brawling and slander, along with every form of malice. Be kind and compassionate to one another, forgiving each other, just as in Christ God forgave you.

45

~⌒~

You are not Forgotten

Suffering can take on a wide variety of faces, but the symptoms are always the same. Suffering is painful, exhausting, draining, all-consuming, and often extremely isolating. But no matter how alone you feel, you aren't. The Lord is ever-present and sees your suffering. And He won't allow it to go on forever. In God's timing, there will be relief, maybe not this side of heaven, but it will come. Until then, He offers His grace to endure. So many situations in this fallen world cause suffering; no one can escape it.

Suffering grows our faith

Thankfully, suffering that God allows is never wasted; it always has a purpose. It yields a harvest for the person who submits to it for the glory of God. As we suffer, our faith can grow. Think of a muscle; it will not grow unless stressed. When muscles undergo intense exercise or weightlifting, the fibers are traumatized which creates an injury. This activates new fibers to repair the damage and form new muscle. Our faith is much the same way; it grows through stress. Suffering creates an injury within us. As we trust God through our suffering, new facets of our faith are activated, creating growth. God is deepening our faith.

Throughout Paul's lifetime of repeated suffering, God promised abundant grace to carry him which was always enough.[1] His grace gave Paul divine strength to persevere. Paul saw hardships and suffering as opportunities to grow closer to the Lord which gave him reason to rejoice, praise, and glorify God.

Suffering opens the door to God's grace for you today as well. Ask Him for the grace to endure and rise above your circumstances. No matter how dark your days seem, the indwelling Holy Spirit provides His grace as a source of strength and comfort that can and will carry you if you trust Him.

Every difficulty is God's opportunity; in fact, sometimes God works best through suffering. Still, it's painful. My best advice: keep walking through the journey. Don't stop and dwell there. Keep moving. God uses every bit of our suffering for our good and for His glory. One step forward at a time. You may even stumble backwards a few steps. That's ok. Get up and walk forward again. We experience spiritual growth through suffering in a way we can't by any other process. Suffering grows our faith in a way that a life of comfort simply cannot.

Suffering prepares us

Suffering is hard, but it prepares us for eternity. In suffering, we are joined to Christ in a special bond, and we become more Christ-like in the process. Interestingly, Christianity has, at its core, the issue of suffering. The cross, a gruesome symbol of execution, is the symbol of our faith. Jesus suffered immensely for us and I'm so glad He did, not taking the easy way out.

As we identify with Him, so must we suffer. Yet within the cross lies His abundant glory. In her book, *Suffering is Never for Nothing*, Elisabeth Elliot would agree. "The deepest things that I have learned in my own life have come from

the deepest suffering. And out of the deepest waters and
the hottest fires have come the deepest things that I know
about God...The greatest gifts of my life have also entailed
the greatest suffering."[A] Suffering can be the means through
which God brings us His greatest blessings as well as eternal
rewards. And He is glorified.

"The present circumstance,
which presses so hard against you
(if surrendered to Christ)
is the best shaped tool in the
Father's hand to chisel you for eternity.
Trust Him, then.
Do not push away the instrument
lest you lose its work."
Max Lucado

There is an eternal purpose tucked within the folds of our
suffering, in the depths we cannot see this side of heaven.

Why must I weep when others sing?
"To test the depths of suffering."

Why must I work while others rest?
"To spend my strength at God's request."

Why must I lose while others gain?
"To understand defeat's sharp pain."

Why must this lot of life be mine
When that which fairer seems is thine?

"Because God knows what plans for me
Shall blossom in eternity."[B]

~L. B. Cowman

Suffering showcases God's power

We are not powerless in our suffering. We can tap into God's infinite power as we lean on Him through prayer and Bible reading. He yearns to help lighten our load to reduce our stress. This world is a shadow—a foretaste—of what's to come: heaven!

So keep walking forward through your valley of suffering. First one step. Then the next. Then the next.

God is using your sufferings in a thousand ways you cannot see. Can you trust Him? Look for glimpses of His glory that remind you He is intimately involved in your life, transforming you in a multitude of ways for your good and His splendor. And one glorious day, when your faith becomes sight, it will all make perfect sense. And you will be eternally grateful He chose you.

God hasn't forgotten you in your valley of suffering; it seems long, but it will end in God's perfect timing. And the joy that follows lasts forever.

May you sense the Lord's loving presence, assuring you of His tender care and covering you with His lavish grace. Press on! You're not alone.

---

[1] 2 Corinthians 12:9a – My grace is sufficient for you.

46

∼⚬∼

Depression

The Great Depression in the United States began in 1929. Lasting about ten years, it plunged the United States, and eventually much of the world, into a panic as banks and businesses closed, wages fell, and buying power tanked. It began after the stock market crash in October of the same year wiped out millions of investors. It soon spread worldwide and was the longest and harshest economic downturn in modern history, resulting in surging rates of poverty and homelessness.

The entire nation moved into a terrible state of emotional depression partly as a result. During that time, the suicide rate in the U.S. was the highest it had ever been and it still holds the record today.[A] Devastating depression descended upon the nation as if a thick, heavy blanket of despair wafted downward, engulfing men, women, and children, robbing them of hope.

Those who grew up during The Great Depression are known as The Greatest Generation. We hear their stories and see how they were changed by crushing hardships during this time. These people developed extreme strength of character as they learned how to survive during these desperate times. They are known for integrity, humility, a strong work ethic, financial shrewdness, extreme loyalty to commitments, and taking personal responsibility for mistakes.

Fast forward almost 100 years

Times sure have changed. Now I believe we are more likely to compromise on honesty and trustworthiness, seek recognition and grandstanding, value entitlement over hard work, spend frivolously while we rack up debt, know not to take people at their word, and blame others for our mistakes.

In another sense, times haven't changed all that much. We still find ourselves in a terrible state of emotional depression. In fact, depression is surging upwards at a staggering rate, especially in teens and young adults. The isolation pervasive with social media use and our addiction to electronic devices seem to be big factors.[B] But there are many causes of depression: addictions, medical issues, genetic propensity, medications, trauma (including physical or sexual abuse), financial debt, sleep disorders, family turmoil, major life events, death, loss, or general life stress.

Of interest, alcohol is a depressant; this is why so many people who struggle with alcohol dependence also struggle with depression, further hindering their ability to cope. Drugs can also exacerbate symptoms of depression.

Two types of depression

In very general terms, there are two different types of depression. There is depression that occurs in response to the stresses of life. We all get sad; sadness is a normal emotion that fades with time. This kind of depression is time-limited and although crippling, the person can still carry on his or her daily routines.

When depression becomes severe, lasting more than few weeks, we should see a doctor to rule out the possibility of a medical cause, such as a hormonal or metabolic imbalance. It is also wise to be assessed by a well-trained clinician (such as a psychiatrist, psychologist, primary care physician, or Christian counselor). There are criteria they can use to determine if our depression is clinical Depression (Major Depressive Disorder) which may benefit from medication or other treatment modalities.

Depression happens to non-Christians and Christians alike. Christians, in fact, are experiencing depression in record numbers. "Depression," according to Dr. Raymond Brown, "is probably the most common human problem."[C] It has been shown that 20-25% of adults will experience major depression during their lifetime.[D] Antidepressant use has increased 64% from 1999 to 2014.[E]

Depression is a common, yet treatable, condition that affects many people worldwide. Yet statistics tell us only about one-third of those with clinical Depression receive treatment. And over two-thirds of suicides reported each year are a result of depression. This is tragic. According to the American Psychiatric Association, "Between 80% and 90% percent of people with depression eventually respond well to treatment. Almost all patients, if they seek help, gain some relief from their symptoms."[F]

Depression has always been with us

Whether or not we have a medical cause or clinical Depression, we should also approach depression from a spiritual standpoint. According to Dr. David Jeremiah, "When depression sets in, faith and hope are often cut loose. With those anchors of the soul gone, it is hard for those suffering from deep despair to rise up and reverse their situations."[G] And Satan will gladly take advantage of this opportunity. He tries to replace our spirit of joy and peace with one of heaviness and fear. If he is successful, he has won a big victory as we will be ineffective for the Kingdom in this state, and for just about everything else.

Having depression doesn't mean a person is lacking in faith or is spiritually immature. Nor is it a result of sin. And getting over depression isn't about "having more faith," or "looking on the bright side." The Bible has much to say about depression, but there is no Bible verse that will "snap us out if it." In fact, many people in the Bible suffered with depression—great men and women of faith like Moses, Jeremiah, Job, Elijah, Jonah, Naomi, etc.

King David, the author of 75 of the 150 Psalms, also battled depression. Many of his Psalms reveal the depths of his depression.

> The cords of death entangled me;
> the torrents of destruction overwhelmed me.
> The cords of the grave coiled around me;
> the snares of death confronted me.
> In my distress I called to the LORD;
> I cried to my God for help.
> From his temple he heard my voice;
> my cry came before him, into his ears.
> Psalm 18:4-6

But here's some encouragement. The Bible promises that when we cry out to God in our despair and sadness, He hears us.

> The righteous cry out,
> and the LORD hears them.
> Psalm 34:17a

His Word tells us what to do.

> Why, my soul, are you downcast? …
> Put your hope in God,
> for I will yet praise him,
> my Savior and my God.
> Psalm 42:5-6

When we are downtrodden, we are told to direct our focus to God and praise Him in our depression—not for the depression, but in the midst of it. For in Him lies our hope. There is always something for which to be thankful. Note how Jeremiah dealt with his depression:

> I remember my affliction and my wandering,
> the bitterness and the gall…
> and my soul is downcast within me.
> Yet this I call to mind
> and therefore I have hope:
> Because of the LORD's great love
> we are not consumed,
> for his compassions never fail.
> They are new every morning;
> great is your faithfulness.
> Lamentations 3:19-23

Some versions say, "His mercies are new every morning." What encouragement!

If you find yourself in a dark place today, know that you're never alone. God knows where you are. He sees your pain and cares deeply. He has good plans for you. Your life is more than your depression. This is not how God designed you to live.

A special caution

Suicide rates are escalating significantly. According to the Centers for Disease Control and Prevention (CDC), suicide is currently the 10th leading cause of death in the United States. It ranks as the second leading cause of death for ages 10-34 and fourth for ages 35-54.[H] The suicide rate increased 35% from 1999 through 2018. In 2018, the suicide rate for males was 3.7 times that of females. From 1999 through 2018, suicide rates among females were highest for ages 45-64; among males, the rates were highest for those ages 75 and up.[I]

Help is available. If you are battling depression, please don't struggle through on your own. Get help. Call someone who understands. Talk to a friend or seek out a professional Christian counselor you can trust.

If suicidal thoughts or tendencies are surfacing, the National Suicide Prevention Hotline at 1-800-273-TALK (8255) is available anytime day or night.

Go online to www.suicidepreventionlifeline.org for more information and help.

Life may be excruciating at times but remember God's great love for us. God's compassion and mercy never fail. He is always faithful.

I would like to extend special thanks to Dr. Kristin Baker for her medical expertise in depressive disorders.

47

Treasures in Darkness

$\mathcal{I}$f you ask ten people with depression to describe it with one word, overwhelmingly one of the most common responses you will hear will be "darkness." Not coincidently, Satan is the prince of darkness. There are over 200 passages in the Bible that address the dark or darkness. It is a very real phenomenon. In this world controlled by the evil one, many people battle the darkness of depression. Job well understood this feeling of despair.

> He has blocked my way so I cannot pass;
> he has shrouded my paths in darkness.
> Job 19:8

Sometimes it feels like wherever we turn, Satan has erected barriers to block our ability to move forward, beyond the darkness. We end up on one detour after another. David experienced this on numerous occasions and turned to God for answers and hope.

> Answer me, O Lord my God;
> give me light in my darkness lest I die.
> Psalm 13:3, TLB

David had it right. He knew where to turn. And God has tucked a ray of hope within the pages of Isaiah.

> I will give you
> treasures of darkness,
> riches stored in secret places,
> so that you may know
> that I am the Lord ...
> who summons you by name.
> Isaiah 45:3

When we are suffering, we don't have the perspective to see that God has provided treasures in the darkness—yet He assures us they are there. God knew we would walk through dark times, so He placed certain riches within the deepest recesses of our pain and sorrow to help us persevere and endure the pain and suffering—as long as we don't isolate ourselves from God. We must allow Him in. This is not misplaced hope; it is the wisest thing we can do.

When tossed about by the fierce storms of depression, God is our "anchor for the soul, firm and secure."[1] He is our solid ground when we falter and stumble in our tears that consume us. He is our strength to persevere through the weariness of long days of suffering.[2] He is our light at the top of the dark pit of despair. And He is our song when no joy remains, rejoicing and singing over us when we have lost our song.[3]

When Jesus Christ died for us, He gave "us new birth into a living hope through the resurrection."[4] We mustn't despair because our hope is alive. Our future is secure. And so is our present.

The darkness will pass so don't give up. And God will use our lives and the suffering with which He's entrusted us for His glory as He brings beauty from the ashes of our depression and a garment of praise instead of a spirit of despair.[5]

Light and darkness

Darkness in our world will not go away completely; this isn't heaven after all. Only in heaven is there pure and complete light and joy. Heaven is God's domain in whom "there is no darkness at all."[6] While living among us, Jesus made an astounding statement: "I am the light of the world!"[7] Known as His second I AM statement, Jesus is proclaiming that He is the light of Truth…the light of eternal life. He is Light itself!

By contrast, Satan is darkness and in him, there is no light; he just "masquerades as an angel of light."[8] He is our enemy—very real and extremely fierce. He will stop at nothing to bring us defeat. Satan hates the light and prefers to do his deeds in darkness. But here's our hope: God is greater than Satan—far greater. And He fights for us every single day. God can turn our darkness into light and bring us treasures in the process.

When walking through depression, we can feel like it has become our identity—like we are of the darkness and the darkness is who we've become. It's important to realize that this simply isn't true. We aren't our depression. Depression is something we're walking through; it has no power to define us.

> You are all children of the light
> and children of the day.
> We do not belong to the night
> or to the darkness.
> 1 Thessalonians 5:5

But we do feel the darkness. In His famous Sermon on the Mount, Jesus says, "If then the light within you is darkness, how great is that darkness!"[9] We are children of light so when darkness invades our hearts through depression, oh how great is that darkness! We feel it deeply.

The darkness, however, has no power against and can never defeat or snuff out the Light of Christ! The apostle Paul offers this wise advice,

> Let your roots grow down into him [Christ],
> and let your lives be built on him.
> Then your faith will grow strong
> in the truth you were taught,
> and you will overflow
> with thankfulness.
> Colossians 2:7, NLT

Prepare ahead of time, during seasons of plenty, seasons of joy, and seasons of laughter. Build your faith now. Memorize verses of the Bible you can pull out when you need them later. These will become hidden treasures to your soul. God's Word encourages us to seek the Light—Jesus. And Jeremiah promises that when we seek Him, we will find Him—always.[10]

Life is short. Heaven is long. The best is yet to come! Do not focus on your despair. You may be tempted to think God has forgotten you. But quite the opposite is true. He is walking each painful step with you. Look to Him. Lean on Him. And seek the treasures of joy God has nestled within the creases of your darkness. When you find them, cherish them, and remember God's goodness with gratitude.

God's glory does shine in the darkness. One day, the sun will burst forth, eclipsing your pain. And the light of His splendor will sparkle with radiance and magnificence too wonderful for words. You will get through this.

1 Hebrews 6:19a

2 Isaiah 40:29 – He gives strength to the weary and increases the power of the weak.

3 Zephaniah 3:17, ESV – The LORD your God is in your midst, a mighty one who will save; he will rejoice over you with gladness; he will quiet you by his love; he will exult over you with loud singing.

4 1 Peter 1:3

5 Isaiah 61:3a – [The LORD has sent me] to bestow on them [those who grieve] a crown of beauty instead of ashes…and a garment of praise instead of a spirit of despair.

6 1 John 1:5b

7 John 8:12a

8 2 Corinthians 11:14

9 Matthew 6:23b

10 Jeremiah 29:13 – You will seek me and find me when you seek me with all your heart.

48

❧

Fighting Depression

*M*any people have argued that depression is a disease of the soul. Dr. David Jeremiah tells us, "Depression has been called the common cold of the soul because most people, sooner or later, catch it."ᴬ Although true, this viewpoint is short-sighted. We are all souls with a body. As such, depression not only impacts our soul, but our physical nature as well. We feel the effects of depression spiritually, emotionally, and physically.

At some point, we will all walk through short periods of depression. Life can be cruel and unrelenting at times. People we love will betray us. Injustices occur. Loved ones die. Tragedies hit and turn our world upside down, sometimes on a moment's notice.

For others of us, depression lasts too long. It grips us and doesn't let go. Along with the sadness, we may also experience fear, anger, a critical spirit, hopelessness, and feelings of being overwhelmed. We may experience panic attacks and difficulty breathing. Tears drench our pillow and hope feels very distant. We feel extremely isolated. We spend a lot of time alone, sleeping more, and often sitting in darkened rooms. When we're fighting depression, we're in the heat of a very real battle.

In both cases, we can feel like we have descended to the depths of a deep pit with our feet stuck in the thick mud at the bottom. All we can see is the sludge and gloomy darkness of the pit of overwhelming despair. Trudging through every day, hour upon hour, it can seem too much to bear. Yet, as Christians, we have a clear advantage; we have somewhere to turn—we can always turn to our Creator. He is the source of our hope.

It's critical we recognize two powerful forces at work.

- Satan is an opportunist, and he takes full advantage of our circumstances to make us feel utterly hopeless and helpless. As believers, we have the Holy Spirit living within us. And He gifts us with spiritual fruit[1] which Satan will try to steal as he can. He especially targets our joy and peace; we mustn't let him win! Resist Satan and his schemes and he will flee.[2] Fight your depression as you would fight temptation or a great injustice. Depression is a very effective tool of Satan, and he wields it well to isolate us from our family, friends, and especially God.

- God is a more powerful force than Satan. He is always with us, looking down from His throne with compassion and love. Jesus sits at the right hand of God, praying for us. God fights for us[3]—constantly shielding, protecting, and strengthening us—even when we're unaware of His presence. We are never left alone to fend for ourselves. We can be successful in rising out of the pit of despair, not in our own puny strength, but in His magnificent strength.[4] Christ has experienced all the anguish we feel and more; He understands. And He promises to meet us in our pain.

Great suffering produces greatness

If you've ever struggled with depression, it may encourage you to know many great men and women of faith have journeyed to the same lonely depths of anguish and depression. They, too, experienced times when God seemed distant and silent to their agonizing pleas for help. Depression seems to be quite common among great theologians. Great suffering, when not wasted, produces greatness.

If you are suffering from depression, you are in excellent company. Look at this list of gifted and exceptional men and women (who as best we can tell are/were Christians) who reportedly suffered depression, some very severe:

Winston Churchill	Charles Dickens
Abraham Lincoln	Florence Nightingale
Charles Spurgeon	George Handel
C.S. Lewis	John Bunyan
Mother Teresa	Isaac Newton
Barbara Bush	Sheila Walsh
Terry Bradshaw	Mel Gibson
Ernest Hemingway	Kevin Sorbo
Martin Luther	Isaac Newton
Pope Francis	Martin Luther King, Jr.
John Calvin	Vincent Van Gogh
John Wesley	Dolly Parton
John James (Newsboys)	Jim Caviezel (played Jesus
William Cowper	in Passion of the Christ)
Mary Beth Chapman	

This list is far from complete. You aren't alone in your suffering. As you struggle with depression, the seeming silence from God, and the tortured anguish, know that God is working to refine, stretch, and shape you into great men and women of faith, if you submit to His will and trust Him in your pain. You may not understand the reason for your suffering, nor perceive that you are changing and growing through it, but you are; a divine transformation is occurring within you. Author Henri Nouwen, a Dutch priest and theologian, explains further, "Our cup is often so full of pain that joy seems completely unreachable. When we are crushed like grapes, we cannot think of the wine we will become."[B]

God is well aware of the battle you are waging and He has not left you, even though His silence may make it seem so. God has an eternal purpose for your life, even if you're fighting depression. In fact, maybe the fact that you're battling depression fits into His grand purpose for your life.

The suffering Servant

No one suffered more than Jesus; he was known as the suffering servant. Isaiah prophesied that Christ would be "a man of suffering, and familiar with pain."[5] As such, Jesus understands our depression, no matter what we are facing. Prior to his crucifixion, he said, "My soul is overwhelmed with sorrow to the point of death."[6] Luke tells us his anguish was so great prior to His crucifixion that "His sweat was like drops of blood falling to the ground."[7]

The greatest truth is this: we have a Savior who understands our pain, who knows our every weakness and hurt, and reaches out with compassion and hope. David tells us, "He lifted me out of the slimy pit."[8] He reaches down and gently lifts us out as well.

God will never waste our seasons of suffering but will use them in some way to bring good, to instill purpose, to help others, and to make us stronger. In God's economy, nothing is ever wasted. And be assured: our suffering is nothing compared to the glory that awaits us in heaven.[9]

Are you suffering? Is your spirit crushed? Are you feeling defeated? Is your heart broken? Even in his darkest, most desperate moments, David remembered that we can always be certain that God hears and acts on our behalf.

The LORD is close to the brokenhearted
and saves those who are crushed in spirit.
Psalm 34:18

Run into the darkness

Grammy and Dove Award winning recording artist Steven Curtis Chapman lost his precious 5-year-old daughter in a tragic accident. She was hit in their driveway of their home by an SUV a family member was driving. In processing their grief, Chapman said, "You can either turn around and run *away* from the darkness, or you can keep running forward. It's counterintuitive and terrifying, but the quickest path to the sunrise is actually to run *into* the darkness."[C]

Never, never, never give up

Britain found themselves in a dire situation. The year was 1940. They faced the brutal and vicious Nazis in war. 340,000 British troops had to escape over the beaches at Dunkirk as the Germans had control of Europe. Their survival seemed impossible.

Out of despair and desperation, the nation turned to Winston Churchill, the Prime Minister of the United Kingdom, for some hope. He gave them a piercing speech, encouraging them to fight with defiance and boldness no matter the cost. "We shall never surrender," he bellowed. "If you're going through hell, keep going." And the charge that led the British from the brink of almost certain defeat to mind-blowing victory on V-E Day (May 8, 1945): "Never, never, never give up."[D]

Keep moving forward

When you're depressed and filled with despair, it feels like you're trudging through the blackest night, unable to see even one step ahead. The natural default is to retreat or try to escape, but you must keep moving forward. You *will* rise above this. In the meantime, know where to turn.

> Let us then approach God's throne of grace
> with confidence, so that we may receive mercy
> and find grace to help us in our time of need.
> Hebrews 4:16

God is with you in the midst of your depression and will fight for you. You are not alone! Admit your depression. Let it come. Face it head on and don't give up. Instead of trying to fight it, try to understand it. What lessons are tucked within the folds of the darkness?

> Even though I walk through the darkest valley,
> I will fear no evil, for you are with me;
> your rod and your staff, they comfort me.
> Psalm 23:4

With God's help, you can persevere through the darkness for this season (a season which *will* end) and glean the harvest, to God's glory, that we can only find through suffering.

Here are a few suggestions to keep you moving forward.

1. Pray often. Worship the Lord who, despite how it may appear, has the universe under control—including your life.
2. Get plenty of sleep.
3. Read your Bible daily.
4. Do not isolate from people. Do not withdraw. Being surrounded by others is therapeutic. It's okay to let others know you hurt.
5. Serve. You may heal more quickly by serving—having a purpose—rather than by receiving.
6. Don't dwell on the whys of your depression. Dwell in the presence of God. Feel your depression; try to understand and find peace with it. Focus on how God can grow you through this challenging time. Rest in Him and trust Him to pull you through.

If none of the above helps, there is no shame in seeking professional help. A good Christian counselor is invaluable.

Suffering from depression isn't the end of the world. God can still use you to do great things for the Kingdom. He redeems our tears as He makes us more like His Son to His glory. There is much honor in that!

Additional Bible Verses to Ponder
when Fighting Depression
(Consider committing some of these to memory.)

Do not be afraid...the LORD
your God himself will fight for you.
Deuteronomy 3:22

———

Today you are going into battle
against your enemies.
Do not be fainthearted or afraid;
do not panic or be terrified by them.
For the LORD your God
is the one who goes with you
to fight for you
against your enemies
to give you victory.
Deuteronomy 20:3-4

———

Be strong and courageous.
Do not be afraid; do not be discouraged,
for the LORD your God
will be with you wherever you go.
Joshua 1:9

———

You, LORD, are my lamp;
the LORD turns my darkness into light.
2 Samuel 22:29

———

My flesh and my heart may fail,
but God is the strength of my heart
and my portion forever.
Psalm 73:26

Those who hope in the LORD
will renew their strength.
They will soar on wings like eagles;
they will run and not grow weary,
they will walk and not be faint.
Isaiah 40:31

So do not fear, for I am with you;
do not be dismayed, for I am your God.
I will strengthen you and help you;
I will uphold you with my righteous right hand.
Isaiah 41:10

If God is for us,
who can be against us?
Romans 8:31b

---

[1] Galatians 5:22-23a, ESV - The fruit of the Spirit is love, joy, peace, patience, kindness, goodness, faithfulness, gentleness, and self-control.

[2] James 4:7b – Resist the devil, and he will flee from you.

[3] Deuteronomy 20:4 – For the Lord your God is the one who goes with you to fight for you against your enemies to give you victory.

[4] Philippians 4:13, NKJV - I can do all things through Christ who strengthens me.

[5] Isaiah 53:3b

[6] Mark 14:34a

[7] Luke 22:44b

[8] Psalm 40:2a

[9] Romans 8:18 - I consider that our present sufferings are not worth comparing with the glory that will be revealed in us.

49

∿

Handel's Messiah

andel's *Messiah* is possibly the most renowned piece of classical music in the world and is an annual tradition for many to usher in the Christmas season. Is there a soul alive who is not moved by the powerful *Hallelujah Chorus*? My husband, Bob, and I were excited to attend *Messiah* at Davidson College one Christmas season. The North Carolina Baroque Orchestra and organ would provide the melodious backdrop to a sing-along led by the very talented Davidson College choirs along with community members from a large surrounding area. I decided to splurge that year and purchase a vocal score of the masterpiece ahead of time so we could sing along with the other avid enthusiasts. After poring through the many selections online, I settled on my choice and placed my order on Amazon.

Many of you, I'm sure, have the Amazon Echo. I enjoy the Echo for a variety of reasons, but one definite plus is the feature that announces the arrival of a package from Amazon. "Refrigerator filter has arrived." "A package, containing suede dog collar, has arrived."

One day, I was tooling about the kitchen when the familiar yellow lighted ring shone from the Echo device. I asked, "Alexa, what's my notification?" Promptly, the device replied, "The Messiah has arrived!" I stopped dead in my tracks, spilling the flour I was measuring. I momentarily forgot to breathe as I froze, processing this new information. My eyes slowly panned the room in the stillness that followed, searching the area carefully. It took a moment to figure out what Alexa was trying to tell me. I had ordered the Handel's *Messiah* musical score two days ago and it had promptly slipped my mind.

When it dawned on me, I broke out laughing!

One day, when we are busy measuring flour, working on a project, bathing the dogs, running errands, or working in the yard, The Messiah surely will return. No one knows when. But I assure you that when this happens, Jesus won't need Alexa to announce His presence. Amazon won't be the first to know. Jesus won't be waiting on our front porch for us to notice His arrival. The world will know in the blink of an eye. Sadly, He will catch many unaware.

> About that day or hour no one knows,
> not even the angels in heaven,
> nor the Son, but only the Father.
> Be on guard! Be alert!
> You do not know when that time will come.
> Mark 13:32-33

Matthew takes this a step further.

> That is how it will be at the coming of the Son of Man.
> Two men will be in the field;
> one will be taken and the other left.
> Two women will be grinding with a hand mill;
> one will be taken and the other left.
> Therefore keep watch, because you do not know
> on what day your Lord will come.
> Matthew 24:39b-42

So you also must be ready,
because the Son of Man will come
at an hour when you do not expect him.
Matthew 24:44

We aren't told when Christ will return. I'm sure God has His reasons. Maybe it's because if we knew the exact day, we might become lazy and non-productive as we wait. Maybe some of us would keep on sinning and living for ourselves until right before He returns, then turn to God in the nick of time. While we wait, we have work to do.

His return is certain; the Bible leaves no room for doubt. It is mentioned in 23 of the 27 New Testament books with over 300 references. All we know is that His return will be unexpected and sudden. There will be no chance for last-minute repentance or negotiations with Jesus. The choice we have already made will determine our eternal destiny.

If the Messiah returns within the hour, will you be ready?

Some interesting history:

George Frideric Handel was born in Halle, Germany on February 23, 1685, into a wealthy family of faith. His father was a renowned surgeon in northern Germany and wanted his son to pursue law.[A] But music stirred his soul. He was a true prodigy and composed dozens of operas during his lifetime. He started quite young. By the time he was ten years old, he had mastered the organ, the oboe, and the violin and he had composed music for all three. From ages eleven to seventeen, Handel composed church cantatas and chamber music.[B] At 18, he composed *Almira*, his first opera.[A]

Handel's compositions were popular with audiences in England, but many detested that he was a foreigner. His rivals made life difficult for him. At one point, his operas lost favor and his health started to fail. "Handel sank into bankruptcy and despair, believing his career was over."[C]

The story behind the composition of *Messiah* is captivating. It was 1741; Handel was invited to Ireland for a charity performance. A deeply religious man, Handel chose to write an oratorio of a totally different kind. It would be all about Christ—His life, death, and resurrection—with an abundance of texts and themes directly from Scripture.[C]

Witnesses said he composed the oratorio with superhuman strength and energy. They thought that "he was mad or under a spell." A servant noted that "Handel seldom ate or slept. He worked with such frenzy that his fingers could no longer hold the pen."[C]

Handel would claim divine inspiration. He created one of the world's great masterpieces in only 24 days—Part 1 in six days, Part 2 in nine days, and Part 3 in six days! The orchestration took only a few more days.[C] The 259-page score contains close to a quarter of a million notes![D] It is said that Handel wept while composing the Hallelujah Chorus; he claimed he saw "visions of angels" during its composition.[E] When he finished this great work, he sobbed, "I think that I did see all heaven before me, and the great God Himself!"[C]

The text for *Messiah* was written by his close friend, Charles Jennens.[D] Part 1 deals with Jesus's birth. Part 2 covers his death and part 3 encompasses His resurrection. Almost all of the lyrics are taken from the Old Testament.

It is pure genius how Jennens was able to tell the story of Jesus's life using texts that preceded his life on earth by hundreds of years![E] At the end of the manuscript, Handel penned the letters *SDG* which stand for *Soli Deo Gloria*, "To God alone the glory."[F]

Messiah made its debut in Dublin, Ireland to a vastly overcrowded audience in April 1742. It was declared a masterpiece.[C] It was meant to be played for Lent as an Easter offering. The Victorians moved it to Christmas to resuscitate enthusiasm in this faltering holiday. The first London performance was a disaster. People felt it was disgraceful to hold this production in a theatre instead of a church. When Handel gave all the proceeds from *Messiah* to charity, the people calmed down.[E]

Legend has it that King George II of England was so moved by the Hallelujah Chorus during the 1743 London premiere that he rose to his feet, prompting the crowd to follow suit.[G] (When the King stands, so does everybody else, according to royal etiquette.) Ever since then, for over 275 years, audiences have continued the tradition!

After his success, Handel continued to write religious music. Then his eyesight began to fail, and he underwent surgery with devastating results: complete blindness. Still, he continued to perform for eight more years until he collapsed while conducting a performance of *Messiah*.[C] He died on April 14, 1759, Holy Saturday, the day before Easter, in his rented house in London, England.[B] He was 74. He was buried in Westminster Abbey. A statue of Handel at his table marks his grave, with the score of *Messiah* opened to the page, "I Know That My Redeemer Liveth."[C]

Handel never married, nor had children. During his lifetime, he composed 29 oratorios (large-scale musical works for orchestra and voices) and 42 operas as well as many other masterpieces.[H] Ludwig van Beethoven claimed, "Handel was the greatest, ablest composer that ever lived."[C] He was a very generous man as well, contributing to many charities, including the Foundling Hospital. He also left money in his will to his servants.[B] Sadly, his fame didn't rise to legendary prominence until after his death.

———

If you want a real treat, google the YouTube video of a flash mob performing Handel's Hallelujah Chorus in the food court of a mall in Welland, Ontario on November 13, 2010. This exceptional and moving performance has been viewed over 55 million times and rising.

Warning: it will give you goose bumps and bring a big smile to your face!

50

The Road to Salvation

*T*he Bible says God has a standard of perfect, unblemished holiness and all of us fall short of this standard because we all sin. It's in our very nature. This applies to every one of us! No one is innocent.

> For all have sinned and
> fall short of the glory of God.
> Romans 3:23

Sin always leads to death—physical death, spiritual death, and eternal death. That's what we deserve because not one of us is righteous (right before God).

> There is no one righteous,
> not even one.
> Romans 3:10

God is totally holy and just; justice must prevail. Justice means sin requires a penalty. Someone must pay to redeem the sin. Since Jesus lived the perfect life, He is the only person who can pay the penalty for our sins so that we don't have to. In His great love for us, God arranged for His Son to buy our freedom, releasing us from the bondage of sin.

Either *we* pay and spend eternity in hell or *Jesus* pays and we spend eternity in heaven. If we don't trade our sin and guilt with Jesus in exchange for His righteousness and unblemished innocence, we must carry the guilt and burden of our sins and live without hope, knowing we face the just penalty for all eternity.

Jesus willingly chose to take our sin on Himself and face the wrath of God, paying the penalty required to redeem us from our sins. The result: we can live eternally in heaven—with Jesus—something we don't deserve. Jesus rescued us from everlasting death. Justice has been served.

> The wages of sin is death,
> but the gift of God is eternal life
> in Christ Jesus our Lord.
> Romans 6:23

It doesn't matter what you've done, nor how far you've strayed from God. He died for all—He died for you.

> God demonstrates his own love for us in this:
> While we were still sinners, Christ died for us.
> Romans 5:8

But it doesn't end in the grave! Jesus rose from the dead; this shows that God accepted His sacrifice as payment for our sins. He put our sins to death on the cross and rose in victory over them.

Your response

God's gift of salvation from sin is offered to everyone but must be accepted. If you believe this Road to Salvation and want to accept this generous and loving gift from God, you must confess that Jesus is Lord of your life and believe in your heart that God raised Jesus from the dead to personally pay for your sins. Then promise to trust in Jesus as your Lord and Savior for the rest of your life.

> If you confess with
> your mouth that Jesus is Lord,
> and believe in your heart that
> God raised him from the dead,
> you will be saved.
> Romans 10:9, ESV

That's all there is to it! If you followed these steps just outlined, you will be saved for eternity! Your sins have been forgiven.

> Everyone who calls on the name
> of the Lord will be saved.
> Romans 10:13

Salvation starts now! It brings us peace with God through Jesus Christ during our life here on earth. The barrier sin created between us and God has been removed. We can have a relationship with Jesus through prayer.

> Since we have been justified through faith,
> we have peace with God
> through our Lord Jesus Christ.
> Romans 5:1

You are loved completely by God, despite your sins. He has forgiven you. When He looks at you, He sees Jesus's righteousness; He doesn't see your sins; you have been cleansed completely.

Though your sins are like scarlet,
they shall be as white as snow.
Isaiah 1:18b

Scarlet was the color of a deep-red dye used by people in Bible times. Its deep, penetrating stain was permanent. Other colors could be bleached out, but not scarlet. The stain of your sins can seem just as permanent; only Christ can forgive you and remove the most unsightly and indelible of sin's stains from your life. God will never bring up your confessed sins. They are gone! He doesn't condemn you. You are forgiven.

There is now no condemnation
for those who are in Christ Jesus.
Romans 8:1

Nothing can ever separate you from God's love for you.

Neither death nor life,
neither angels nor demons,
neither the present nor the future,
nor any powers, neither height nor depth,
nor anything else in all creation,
will be able to separate us
from the love of God that
is in Christ Jesus our Lord.
Romans 8:38-39

If you agree with the Road to Salvation outlined on the previous pages, here is a simple prayer you can pray right now. Say this prayer out loud to reflect the faith you now have in Jesus Christ.

———

"Lord Jesus, I know that I am a sinner and every sin I commit is against You. Please forgive me. I believe You paid for my sins by taking the punishment that I deserve. You died for my sins, then rose from the dead. I turn from my sins and the life I have been living. I invite You to come into my heart and my life. I place my trust in You for salvation. I want to trust and follow You as my Lord and Savior and worship You as King of kings and Lord of lords. Thank You for the gift of eternal life in heaven. Amen."

———

If you prayed that prayer, reach out and tell someone. Find a church and start attending regularly. Buy a Bible and start reading it every day. Join a Sunday School class or a small group at church. And it would bless me greatly to know of your decision. Would you be so kind to let me know? Please email me at: kimskinneybooks@gmail.com.

Congratulations. You have made a monumental decision today. Write down this date. You'll remember this moment always.

Today, on _____ I profess my
(today's date)
faith in Jesus Christ.

_____
(your signature)

Closing Prayer

Holy God,

You are the essence of glory. You are filled with glory and You emanate glory. Absolutely everything You created reverberates with Your glory.

Who are we that You made us in your image? Within the core of our being, You planted seeds of divine glory. As we water these seeds with faith, lavish us with Your grace and love so that our lives radiate Your glory and majesty no matter what challenge we face, no matter what the future holds. In You lie our joy and confidence for today, our hope for a tomorrow brimming with promise, and an eternal future bursting with resplendent glory.

We praise You and we magnify Your holy name.

Amen.

Notes

Introduction

    A.   Facebook post by Paul David Tripp from July 21, 2012.

Chapter 1 – One Story

    A.   Lawson, S. (2016, June 29). Fulfilled prophecy demonstrates the divine inspiration of scripture. Ligonier Communications. https://www.ligonier.org/posts/fulfilled-prophecy-demonstrates-divine-inspiration-scripture

Chapter 2 – Our Integrity is our Legacy

    A.   Laurie, G. (2008, March 20). *What's Inside?* Harvest. https://harvest.org/resources/devotion/whats-inside-2/

    B.   Sanders, A. (1998). *I'm trying to number my days, but I keep losing count!* (1st ed.). Colorado Springs, CO: WaterBrook Press. p. 121.

Chapter 4 – Sudden Storms

    A.   Author unknown

Chapter 5 – Imprisoned

A.   *Book of 2 Timothy Explained.* (n.d.). Discover the books of the Bible. Bible-studys.org. https://www.biblestudys.org/Bible%20Books/2%20Timothy/Book%20of%202%20Timothy.html

B.   Jeter, D. G. (2017, August 14). *Historical background of Paul's final imprisonment.* Insight for Living. https://www.insight.org/resources/article-library/individual/historical-background-of-paul-s-final-imprisonment

C.   Apablaza, S. (n.d.) *Conditions of Prisons in the First Century: Paul in Roman Custody.* Scribd. https://www.scribd.com/doc/14354155/Life-in-Prison-in-1ad

D.   Powell, M. A. (2018). *Supplement to Introducing the Testament: A Historical, Literary, and Theological Survey,* 2nd ed. ©. Ada, Michigan: Baker Academic. http://cdn.bakerpublishinggroup.com/processed/es ourceassets/files/1960/original/23.6.Prison_Conditi ons_in_the_Roman_World.pdf?1525182932

E.   Swindoll, C. R. (2010). *Insight's New Testament handbook.* Plano, TX: IFL Publishing House. p. 67

F.   *Archaeological Study Bible*, New International Version. (2005). Grand Rapids, MI: Zondervan. p. 1969.

G.   Jackson, W. (2021, May 4). Was Paul's Reference to His Cloak a meaningless triviality? *Christian Courier.* https://www.christiancourier.com/articles/935-was-pauls-reference-to-his-cloak-a-meaningless-triviality

H.   Oakes, J. (2005, December 4). *Were people literate in the time of Jesus?* Evidence for Christianity. https://evidenceforchristianity.org/were-people-literate-in-the-time-of-jesus-r/

Chapter 7 — But Even if He Does Not...

A. Creutzfeldt-Jakob Disease Fact Sheet. (2020, March 13). National Institute of Neurological Disorders and Stroke. Creutzfeldt-Jakob Disease Fact Sheet | National Institute of Neurological Disorders and Stroke (nih.gov)
B. The Reimann family. (2013, December 18). *Jim Reimann*. JimReimann.com. https://jimreimann.com/biography/from-the-family/

Chapter 8 — Complacency is Deadly

A. Levine, A. (2014). *On the edge: Leadership lessons from Mount Everest and other extreme environments.* New York, NY: Grand Central Publishing. pp. 89-90.
B. Ibid. pp. 90-91.
C. Ibid. pp. 87-88.
D. Ibid. p. 83.
E. Ibid. pp. 78-79.
F. Kell, G. (2015, May 26). *The pattern among fallen pastors.* The Gospel Coalition. https://www.thegospelcoalition.org/article/the-pattern-among-fallen-pastors/.
G. Mercer, K. (2020, August 16). *"Called up to lead."* Sermon presented at Two Cities Church, Winston-Salem, NC.

Chapter 9 – Overcoming Complacency

A.   Penley, P. (2016, June 17). *"I wish you were cold or hot, not lukewarm" doesn't mean Jesus prefers you hate him instead of "live on the fence."* Reenacting the Way (of Jesus). https://www.reenactingtheway.com/blog/i-wish-you-were-cold-or-hot-not-lukewarm-doesnt-mean-jesus-prefers-you-hate-him-instead-of-live-on-the-fence6135488

B.   Le Peau, A. (2014, January 28). *A lukewarm interpretation of hot and cold: Revelation 3:15-16.* Andy Unedited. https://andyunedited.com/2014/01/28/a-lukewarm-interpretation-of-h/#:~:text=%E2%80%9CBecause%20you%20are%20lukewarm%E2%80%93neither,most%20misused%20in%20the%20Bible.

Chapter 11 – Run Toward Victory!

A.   Wiersbe, W. (2007). The Wiersbe Bible Commentary: the complete Old Testament in one volume. David C. Cook: Colorado Springs, CO. p. 522.

B.   Metcalf, T. (2016, June 14). Whistling Sling Bullets Were Roman Troops' Secret Weapon Soldiers. LiveScience. https://www.scientificamerican.com/article/whistling-sling-bullets-were-roman-troops-secret-weapon/#:~:text=Deadly%20in%20expert%20hands&text=In%20the%20hands%20of%20an,your%20head%2C%22%20Reid%20said.

Chapter 12 – The Salmon Run

A.   Beach MH (1984). "Fish pass design – criteria for the design and approval of fish passes and other structures to facilitate the passage of migratory fish in rivers". *Fish Res Tech Rep.* 78: 1-46.

B.   Salmon run. (n.d.). In *Wikipedia*. https://en.wikipedia.org/wiki/Salmon_run.

C.   *What salmon eat and what eats salmon*. (n.d.) Bureau of Land Management. https://www.blm.gov/or/resources/recreation/mcgregor/files/what_salmon_eat.pdf.

D.   Dybdal, D. (2011, September 23). *Salmon can 'sniff out' predators*. Fishfarming Expert. https://www.fishfarmingexpert.com/article/salmon-can-sniff-out-predators/

E.   *Cumulative impacts to salmon*. (n.d.) Raincoast Conservation Foundation. https://www.raincoast.org/wp-content/uploads/Cumulative-threats-to-salmon.pdf.

Chapter 13 – Two Seas

A.   Creasong, J. (2008, April 8). *There are two major bodies of water in the land...* Sermon Central. https://www.sermoncentral.com/sermon-illustrations/66112/there-are-two-major-bodies-of-water-in-the-land-by-sermon-central.

B.   Dodson, B. (2009, November 18). *Sea of Galilee vs. the Dead Sea*. Acts 242 Study. https://acts242study.com/sea-of-gallilee-vs-the-dead-sea/.

C.   Fraser, R. (2018, January 25). Are you like the Dead Sea or the Sea of Galilee? *Jackson Sun*. https://www.jacksonsun.com/story/opinion/columnists/2018/01/25/you-like-dead-sea-sea-galilee/1065659001/.

D.   Pletcher, K. (2020). Dead Sea. A. Augustyn (Ed.), *Encyclopaedia Brittanica*. https://www.britannica.com/place/Dead-Sea.

E. *10 interesting facts about the Dead Sea.* (2019, May 14). On the Go Tours. https://www.onthegotours.com/blog/2019/05/fact s-about-the-dead-sea/

F. Frazer, J. (2011, October 9). *Fountains of life found at the bottom of the Dead Sea.* Scientific American. https://blogs.scientificamerican.com/artful-amoeba/fountains-of-life-found-at-the-bottom-of-the-dead-sea/

Chapter 14 – Blessed Be the Name of the Lord

A. Swindoll, C. (2013, April 11). Holding on Loosely. Insight for Living Ministries. https://www.insight.org/resources/article-library/individual/holding-on-loosely

Chapter 16 – Three Trees and Three Gardens

A. Sleeth, M. (2019, April 12). What is the significance of trees in the Bible? Why did Jesus die on a tree? Christianity.com. https://www.christianity.com/wiki/jesus-christ/what-is-the-significance-of-trees-in-the-bible-why-did-jesus-die-on-a-tree.html

B. Coder, K. (2016, October). Trees of the Bible: A cultural history. Warnell Outreach. https://bugwoodcloud.org/resource/files/15224.pdf

Chapter 17 – Born Twice – Die Once

A. Jeremiah, D. (2013). *What are you afraid of: Facing down your fears with faith.* Carol Stream, IL: Tyndale House Publishers, Inc. p. 228.

Chapter 20 – Never Touch the Glory

A. Murray, A. (2015). *Humility*. CreateSpace Independent Publishing Platform.
B. This quote is taken from Chuck Swindoll's message: *The glory of God*. (Swindoll is pastor and founder of Insight for Living Ministries.) https://insight.org/broadcasts/player/?bid=2609&start=.1&preview=6/16/2016&ga=insights_to_share
C. Wiersbe, W. (1993). *Wiersbe's expository outlines on the Old Testament*. Elgin, IL: David C. Cook, p. 556.
D. Graham, B. (2007). *Billy Graham, God's ambassador: A celebration of his life and ministry*. New York, NY: Harper One, p. 173.

Chapter 21 – It is Well with My Soul

A. Maxey, A. (2008, January 11). *Reflections: Horatio G. Spafford, Jr.* http://www.zianet.com/maxey/reflx331.htm.
B. *Isabella's uncle and the hymn that changed America.* (n.d.). Isabella Alden. https://isabellaalden.com/2017/08/22/isabellas-uncle-and-the-hymn-that-changed-america/
C. Fenner, C. & Bumgardner, C. (2018, July 5). *It is well with my soul*. Hymnology Archive. https://www.hymnologyarchive.com/it-is-well-with-my-soul
D. *It is well with my soul*. (2012, October 24). Latter Days Ministry. https://www.hymnologyarchive.com/it-is-well-with-my-soul

E. *Horatio Gates Spafford – The story behind the hymn "It is well with my soul."* (2018, December 12). Bethel Church Ripon. https://www.bethelripon.com/life-stories/horatio-gates-spafford#:~:text=The%20music%2C%20which%20was%20written,malaria%20on%2016th%20October%201888.&text=It%20can%20truly%20be%20said,is%20well%20with%20their%20souls.%E2%80%9D.

F. History.com Editors. (2018, August 21). *Chicago fire of 1871*. History.com. https://www.history.com/topics/19th-century/great-chicago-fire.

G. *Horatio Spafford: It is Well with My Soul.* (2010, June 11). Christianity.com. https://www.christianity.com/church/church-history/timeline/1801-1900/horatio-spafford-it-is-well-with-my-soul-11633070.html

H. Hawkins, S. (2006, September 11). *God's Comfort: It is well with my soul.* Bible.org. https://bible.org/seriespage/6-god-s-comfort-it-well-my-soul.

I. Awful collision in the Atlantic. (1873, December 2). *The Dundee Courier and Argus.* p. 3 https://static1.squarespace.com/static/5b11858da2772cf01402ee6e/t/5f0373e1ddb2f061ae651f97/1594061812990/Dundee_Courier_and_Argus_Dec_2_1873_page3.jpg.

J. Vester, B. S. (1951). *Our Jerusalem.* New York, NY: Doubleday Publishing. p. 56

K. Ibid. pp. 55-56.

L. *Horatio Spafford's Second Chapter.* (n.d.). Isabella Alden.
    https://isabellaalden.com/2017/08/28/horatio-
    spaffords-second-chapter/
M. *Horatio Spafford.* (n.d.). Friends of Zion Museum.
    https://www.fozmuseum.com/explore-foz/horatio-
    spafford/.

Photo Credits

aa. Wikipedia, public domain.
bb. Photo courtesy of The Library of Congress Digital
    IC ppmsca.07650. Circa 1873.
    https://www.loc.gov/exhibits/americancolony/amc
    olony-family.html#obj5
cc. Photo courtesy of The Library of Congress.
dd. Image courtesy of Manuscript Division of The
    Library of Congress(6). Circa 1873.
    https://www.loc.gov/exhibits/americancolony/amc
    olony-family.html#obj6
ee. Wikimedia Commons, public domain

Chapter 22 – Do You Want to Get Well?

A. MacArthur, J. (2005). *The MacArthur Bible commentary.*
    Nashville, TN: Thomas Nelson, Inc. p. 1368.
B. Miller, D. (2007). *The Stirring of the Water and Bible
    Integrity.* Apologetics Press.
    http://apologeticspress.org/APContent.aspx?catego
    ry=13&article=2103.

Chapter 23 – Getting Well

A. Hybels, Bill. (2008). *Too busy not to pray.* (3rd ed.).
    Downer's Grove, IL: Intervarsity Press. p. 101.

Chapter 24 – Be There—Nothing Else Matters

A.   Pistol Pete' Maravich, 40, dies of heart attack at game. (1988,   January 6). *The Orlando Sentinel.* https://www.orlandosentinel.com/news/os-xpm-1988-01-06-0010050036-story.html.

B.   Crowe, J. (2007, June 18). Pickup game with legend ended with a tragic death. *Los Angeles Times.* https://www.latimes.com/archives/la-xpm-2007-jun-18-sp-crowesnest18-story.html.

C.   Summers, D. (2020, January 15). There will never be another Pistol Pete. *Pikes Peak Newspapers.* https://gazette.com/woodmenedition/there-will-never-be-another-pistol-pete-from-the-sidelines/article_eb56cba2-330d-11ea-9995-8bdb24a0fc2f.html.

D.   *Dobson to Graduates: "Be there."* (1997, May 22). Huntington University. https://www.huntington.edu/news/dobson-to-graduates-be-there.

Chapter 25 – Whose Glory?

A.   Tim Tebow's shocking story about John: 3:16. (2018, January 7). *CBN News.* https://www1.cbn.com/cbnnews/entertainment/2018/january/tim-tebow-rsquo-s-nbsp-shocking-story-about-john-3-16-lsquo-coincidence-rsquo-goes-viral.

B.   Elder, L. (2012, January 12 and updated 2017, August 28). Tim Tebow has magic numbers in 3, 1, 6. *Daily News.* https://www.dailynews.com/2012/01/12/larry-elder-tim-tebow-has-magic-numbers-in-3-1-6/.

C. DiRocco, M. (2010, April 17). The message is out on eye black in college football and the NFL. *The Florida Times-Union: Jacksonville.* https://www.jacksonville.com/article/20100417/SPORTS/801253940.

D. Martin, D. (2010, February 3). *Top 5 Tim Tebow eye black biblical verses.* The Christian Science Monitor. https://www.csmonitor.com/USA/Society/2010/0203/Top-5-Tim-Tebow-eye-black-biblical-verses.

E. Halloran, K. (2012, March 19). *11 Bible verses on Tim Tebow's eye black.* Unlocking the Bible. https://unlockingthebible.org/2012/03/11-bible-verses-on-tim-tebows-eye-black/.

F. Lewis, T. (2019, January 14.) Tim Tebow's eye black Bible verses: A guide. *The Times-Picayune.* https://www.al.com/press-register-sports/2009/12/tim_tebows_eye_black_bible_ver.html.

Chapter 26 – Unshakable Peace

A. Chambers, O. (1992). *My Utmost for His Highest.* Grand Rapids, MI: Discovery House Publishers.

Chapter 28 – I am Worn Out Because...

A. Wiersbe, W. (2007). *The Wiersbe Bible Commentary: The Complete Old Testament in One Volume.* Colorado Springs, CO: David C. Cook. p. 1185.

Chapter 31 – Count the Cost

A. Niles, R. (2017, March 6.) *Jericho and Jesus.* Drive Thru History. https://drivethruhistory.com/jericho-and-jesus/

B. Cloak. (n.d.). *King James Bible Dictionary.* http://kingjamesbibledictionary.com/Dictionary/cloak

Chapter 33 – On Fire

A. *What does it mean to walk in the Spirit?* Got Questions Ministry. What does it mean to walk in the Spirit? | GotQuestions.org

B. Wiersbe, W. (2007). *The Wiersbe Bible commentary: The complete New Testament in one volume.* Colorado Springs, CO: David C. Cook. p. 508.

C. Ramsay, W. (1875). Triumphus. *A Dictionary of Greek and Roman Atiquities.* John M. Murray, London. p. 1163-1167. https://penelope.uchicago.edu/Thayer/E/Roman/Texts/secondary/SMIGRA*/Triumphus.html

Chapter 38 – Battles

A. Dye, Ginny. (2013). The Last Long Night: 1864-1865. Bellingham, WA: Bregdan Publishing, p. 107.

Chapter 39 – Fighting Giants

A. Swindoll, C. R. (1997). *A man of passion & destiny: David.* Nashville, TN: W Publishing Group, a Division of Thomas Nelson, Inc. p. 44.

B. Ibid. p. 48.

Chapter 40 – The Armor of God

A. Wickstrom, S. P. (2018) *Ephesians 6:10-18: The Armor of God.* Christian Articles by Steven P. Wickstrom. http://www.spwickstrom.com/armor/

B. Warren, J. & Warren, L. Word of his Hand. (n.d.). *Put on the full armor of God.* [Pamphlet].

C. Johnson, D. (2021) *What is the breastplate of righteousness?* Life Hope & Truth. https://lifehopeandtruth.com/change/christian-conversion/armor-of-god/breastplate-of-righteousness/

D. Padfield, D. (n.d.) *Is the armor too heavy?* The Church of Christ in Zion, Illinois. https://www.padfield.com/1995/armor-of-god.html

E. Myers, J. (n.d.). *Taking up the shield of faith.* Redeeming God. https://lifehopeandtruth.com/change/christian-conversion/armor-of-god/breastplate-of-righteousness/

F. *Professing faith: Bible uses Roman armor to symbolize spiritual armor.* (2016, November 16). Redlands Daily Facts. https://www.redlandsdailyfacts.com/2016/11/16/profe ssing-faith-bible-uses-roman-armor-to-symbolize-spiritual-armor/

G. Johnson, D. (2021). *What is the helmet of salvation?* Life Hope & Truth. https://lifehopeandtruth.com/change/christian-conversion/armor-of-god/helmet-of-salvation/

H. Graham, B. (2009, September). *You can overcome temptation.* Decision Magazine. pp 2-5.

Chapter 41 – A Holy Fruit Basket

A. Bonhoeffer, D. (2012). *The cost of discipleship.* New York, NY: Touchstone.

B. Lewis, C. S. (1955). *Surprised by Joy: The shape of my early life.* New York, NY: Harcourt Brace Jovanovich.

Chapter 43 – The Swab Test

A. Helmenstine, A. M. (2019, November 19). *Common Chemicals That Could Give a False Positive TSA Swab Test.* ThoughtCo. https://www.thoughtco.com/ chemicals-false-positive-tsa-swab-test-606808

Chapter 45 – You Aren't Forgotten

A. Elliot, E. (2019). *Suffering is never for nothing.* Nashville, TN: B&H Publishing Group. p. 9.

B. Cowman, L. B. (2021, March 7). *Streams in the desert.* Crosswalk.com. https://www.crosswalk.com/devotionals/desert/str eams-in-the-desert-march-7th.html

Chapter 46 – Depression

A. Ducharme, J. (2019, June 20). U.S. Suicide rates are the highest they've been since World War II. *Time Magazine.* https://time.com/5609124/us-suicide-rate-increase/

B. Fox, M. (2018, May 10). Major depression on the rise among everyone, new data shows. *NBC Health News.* https://www.nbcnews.com/health/health-news/major-depression-rise-among-everyone-new-data-shows-n873146.

C. Brown R. (2003, July). *Elijah: The problem of depression.* Wycliff Associates. https://www.easyenglish.bible/problems/tpaou07-pbw.htm.

D. Bhandari, S. reviewer (2020). *Major depression (Clinical depression).* WebMD. https://www.webmd.com/depression/guide/major-depression#1.

E. Winerman, L. (2017, November). *By the numbers, antidepressant use on the rise.* American Psychological Association. https://www.apa.org/monitor/2017/11/numbers.

F. Torres, F. (2020, October). *What is depression?* American Psychiatric Association. https://www.psychiatry.org/patients-families/depression/what-is-depression

G. Jeremiah, D. (2013) *What are you afraid of: Facing down your fears with faith.* Carol Stream, IL: Tyndale House Publishers. p. 204.

H. *Ten leading causes of death and Injury.* (2018). Centers for Disease Control and Prevention. https://www.cdc.gov/injury/wisqars/LeadingCauses_images.html.

I. Hedegaard, H, Curtin, S.C., & Warner, M. (2020, April). *Increase in suicide mortality in the United States, 1999-2018.* NCHS Data Brief No. 362. US Department of Health and Human Services. https://www.nimh.nih.gov/health/statistics/suicide.shtml

Chapter 48 – Fighting Depression

A.   Jeremiah, D. (2013) *What are you afraid of: Facing down your fears with faith*. Carol Stream, IL: Tyndale House Publishers. p. 200.

B.   Nouwen, H. (2006). *Can you drink the cup?* Notre Dame, IN: Ave Maria Press. p. 51.

C   Stoneman, T. (2010, April). Signs of Spring. *In Touch Magazine*. Volume 33 (No. 4). p. 14.

D.   Loftus, G. (2012, May 9). If you're going through hell, Keep going - Winston Churchill. *Forbes Magazine*. https://www.forbes.com/sites/geoffloftus/2012/05/09/if-youre-going-through-hell-keep-going-winston-churchill/?sh=3fc9c05ed549

Chapter 49 – Handel's Messiah

A.   Kandell, J. (2009, December). The Glorious History of Handel's Messiah. *Smithsonian Magazine*. https://www.smithsonianmag.com/arts-culture/the-glorious-history-of-handels-messiah-148168540/

B.   Biography.com Editors. (2014, July 21. Updated 2020, June 16). *George Frideric Handel Biography*. Biography.com. https://www.biography.com/musician/george-handel

C.   Colson, C. (2000, December 22). *Handel's Masterpiece*. Breakpoint Colson Center. https://breakpoint.org/handels-masterpiece/

D.   O'Bannon, R. (n.d.). *5 things you might not know about Handel's Messiah*. Baltimore Symphony Orchestra. https://www.bsomusic.org/stories/5-things-you-might-not-know-about-handels-messiah/

E. Harris, R. (2015, December 6). *Handel's Messiah: 6 surprising facts.* CBCRadio-Canada. https://www.cbc.ca/news/entertainment/handel-s-messiah-6-surprising-facts-1.3351122

F. Fun facts about Handel's 'Messiah'. (2015, December 10). *Tenessean.* https://www.tennessean.com/story/entertainment/2015/12/10/fun-facts-handels-messiah/77046392/

G. *10 things you (probably) didn't know about Handel's Messiah.* (2019, August 9). Orchestra of the Age of Enlightenment. https://oae.co.uk/10-things-you-probably-didnt-know-about-handels-messiah/

H. *George Frideric Handel.* (n.d.). Philadelphia Chamber Music Society. https://www.pcmsconcerts.org/composer/george-frideric-handel/

Topical Index
(Organized by chapter title number, not page number)

～

Meet the Author

~❧~

$\mathcal{K}$im S. Kinney was born in Yankton, South Dakota and lived a short while in Winner, a small rural town in the middle of the state. She mostly grew up in Glendale, Wisconsin and has been involved with ministry her whole life. She started teaching Sunday School at age fifteen to a large, rambunctious class of 2nd grade boys that no one else wanted (who locked her out of the classroom on her very first day). Her passion is creatively teaching God's Word to young adults and women of all ages.

In 2005, she launched and led an online ministry for young adults and professionals. It quickly grew and boasted a presence in eight different countries. It was during these years that the Lord birthed in her the desire to write.

She and her husband, Bob, make their home in Kannapolis, North Carolina. They have two grown children. Justin (J. Robert) lives in Knoxville, TN and is an avid, award-winning writer of Christian suspense thrillers. Rebecca lives in Winston-Salem, NC and pours her writing talents into research papers.

Kim is active in church, the community, and with an international anti-human trafficking ministry. She enjoys spending time with her family and their dogs, writing, reading, cycling, swimming, participating in anything water-related, and adventuring in the outdoors.

~❧~

Connect with me

It has been my great privilege to share this first book in *The Glory Series* with you. I pray it blessed you in some way. If you have enjoyed this book, a short review posted on Amazon and/or Goodreads would be very much appreciated. These reviews are invaluable to authors.

It would be fun for me to know your favorite chapter(s), topic(s), and/or writing styles. Your comments will be very helpful as I continue to write.

You can connect with me in various ways:
Email: kimskinneybooks@gmail.com
Facebook and Instagram: @KimSKinneyauthor
Website: kimskinneybooks.wixsite.com/glory
Amazon author page: amazon.com/author/kimskinney

Free Gift

When you sign up on my website for occasional emails to be notified of upcoming book releases or other news, you will receive a free gift: 42 beautiful inspirational quote cards. All quotes are taken from *Living For His Glory*. kimskinneybooks.wixsite.com/glory

Living for His *Glory*